Additional Praise for Friends on a Rotten Day

"I came away from reading *Friends on a Rotten Day* with a whole new understanding of the term "kindred spirits." The more I learn about star signs, the more helpful they are for choosing both girl-friends ... and boyfriends! Thanks, Hazel, for a terrific book—I'm buying copies for all my soul sisters!"
　—BJ Gallagher, author of *Friends Are Everything*

"Light-hearted, witty, entertaining, and surprisingly insightful and illuminating in terms of describing the traits and proclivities, both positive and negative, of the twelve signs of the zodiac. Readers will definitely recognize themselves and their friends."
　—Damian Sharp, author of *Learning Astrology*

"Like Drew Barrymore (Pisces), I (Aquarius) also grew up with the *Cosmo Bedside Astrologer* Annual as my bible and compass for navigating life. I love Hazel Dixon-Cooper's (Pisces) *Born on a Rotten Day* book so much, I permanently borrowed (accidentally stole) one from a Leo publicist—NEVER a good idea! *Friends on a Rotten Day* is a deliciously naughty peek into the secret life of friendships and gives some great, common sense advice, too!"
　—Varla Ventura, author of *Wild Women Talk About Love* and
　　Sheroes

"Hazel Dixon-Cooper has found an innovative way to let us know about the highs and lows of friendships according to the astrological signs. Her snappy prose is engaging and her astrological insights very perceptive. This is a new focus for astrology and well worth reading."
　—Constance Stellas, author of *The Everything Sex Signs Book*

"Amazingly accurate, brilliantly written, this is the definitive book on friendship. Hazel Dixon-Cooper is the funniest woman on the planet, and *Friends on a Rotten Day* is her best book yet."
—Bonnie Hearn Hill, author of the Geri LaRue newspaper thriller series

Also by Hazel Dixon-Cooper

Born on a Rotten Day:
Illuminating and Coping with the
Dark Side of the Zodiac (2002)

Love on a Rotten Day:
An Astrological Survival Guide
to Romance (2004)

FRIENDS ON A ROTTEN DAY

the Astrology of friendships

HAZEL DIXON-COOPER

WEISER BOOKS
San Francisco, CA / Newburyport, MA

First published in 2008 by
Red Wheel/Weiser, LLC
With offices at:
500 Third Street, Suite 230
San Francisco, CA 94107
www.redwheelweiser.com

Library of Congress Cataloging-in-Publication Data
Dixon-Cooper, Hazel
  Friends on a rotten day : the astrology of friendships / Hazel Dixon-Cooper.
      p. cm.
  ISBN 978-1-57863-412-5 (alk. paper)
  1. Zodiac—Miscellanea. 2. Astrology. 3. Friendship—Miscellanea.
I. Title.
  BF1726.D59 2008
  133.5'815825--dc22

                              2007037769

Cover and text design by Donna Linden
Typeset in Perpetua and Tree-Boxelder
Cover illustration © Roxanna Bikadoroff
Text illustrations © Christian Naud/iStockphoto.com

Printed in Canada
TCP
10 9 8 7 6 5 4 3 2 1

FOR YOU, GIRLFRIEND.

"Good friends will help you move.
Best friends will help you move the bodies."
UNKNOWN

Contents

Acknowledgments

Special thanks and appreciation to these old and new friends:

June Clark, the best agent in the Universe, for her tireless energy and support

My editor, Brenda Knight, for her kind encouragement and the suggestions that made this a better book

The Tuesdays, the best writing group anywhere, and

Bonnie Hearn-Hill, Sheree Petree, Ryan Booth, Evan Piercy, Chris Poe, and the inspiring, irreverant Fridays.

Introduction

Never break a date with a girlfriend to go out with a man.
UNKNOWN

Kindred Spirits

"I know just what you mean." How many times have you said, or heard, these words? Whether you're sharing the latest hot topic or discussing the strange behavior patterns of men, no one understands you as well as your girlfriends. Women friends come in a wide variety—childhood friend, college roommate, coworker, neighbor, sister, and mother. On good days, rotten days, and every day between, a friend is always there to listen, comfort, and encourage.

It's easy to make friends with someone you instantly like. You know, when you get that *seems like we've known each other forever* feeling when you first meet. Others are more challenging. You don't think alike. Maybe she likes to plan ahead while you're more spontaneous. Is it impossible to make a forever friendship? Of course not. The key is knowing why she acts in a certain way. Learn that, and you'll have an edge in making woman-to-woman relationships that last.

Astrology tells us that being soulmates is not limited to romantic relationships. According to relationship experts, friendship can be as significant in our lives as love. From ancient times to today, women have connected through talk. Then, it might have been a whispered conversation in the harem. Today, perhaps it's a wine-and-vent session after work. Throughout the ages, women have forged an emotional bond of empathy that has upheld, nurtured, and provided definition to our lives. This female bond has helped to lay the groundwork for everything from social revolution to personal transformation. Girlfriends are our collaborators for change. Who else do we tell our secret wishes, dangerous desires, and most private dreams? Who else helps us to plot, plan, and unleash our feminine power?

You know your friends well. But imagine knowing them even better. Ever wonder why your Gemini buddy changes her mind so often? Or your Virgo gal pal sweats the small stuff? It's more than a personal quirk. Learning about her Sun sign will give you insight into what makes her tick on a soul level.

In this book you'll discover why a Scorpio girlfriend sometimes seems distant, a Leo chum needs frequent head pats, and a Libra pal should never be forced to make a snap decision. You'll learn why a Capricorn girlfriend might seem too serious for her own good, uncover the truth about a Taurus friend's hidden anxieties or an Aries chum's competitive side. You'll understand what causes Cancer pal's emotional train wrecks and why your Pisces pal sometimes seems like she's from another planet; the real reasons behind an Aquarius buddy's rebellious side and a Sagittarius girlfriend's occasional angry outburst.

What about those less-than-perfect relationships? Think you can't ever get along with Mom or your sister, or like that friend-of-a-friend who's on the outer fringes of your inner circle? Not true. Knowing a few essential traits of her Sun sign can make that connection stronger. As a bonus, it will enable you to spot the phony behavior patterns of those backstabbers and man stealers who occasionally cross our paths.

My girlfriends and I sometimes talk about living close together when we are old. Maybe we would buy houses on the same street at the beach or connecting condos in the city. The men in our lives are always secondary to this plan of ensuring that we remain close within the safety net of our comforting female friendship. Guys may be there, but the real bond won't let space or time or age disconnect our ties.

Lovers come and go, spouses can't quite figure us out, and the kids grow up and leave home. Our girlfriends never stop sustaining, nurturing, and protecting us. Whether she's a funny, sometimes flaky Gemini, a loyal-but-secretive Scorpio, or an exuberant, self-centered Aries, learning about her Sun sign will help you to gain a new understanding of every woman in your life.

What about the Guys?

Guyfriend might seem like an oxymoron. Yet, you can be platonic pals with a man, once you get past the sex. Attraction between women and men is an unavoidable law of nature. We've all met guys we'd love to know *that* way but they aren't attracted to us, and we've all had guys we would like to get to know, but not in the biblical sense, who had a crush on us. This dance of the sexes takes different forms, such as the ones listed here:

- *Someday:* Either you or he has the crush and hope that if you hang around long enough, it will be reciprocated.
- *Never:* You want him or he wants you. However, the other person's feelings range from I'm-flattered-but-sorry to no-way-in-hell, baby.
- *Timing:* You, he, or both are committed or married to someone else. Anything more than friendship is off limits and/or a disaster waiting to happen.
- *He's gay:* Even if you're a little heartbroken, look on the bright side. You can take him anywhere (even shopping, as he usually has great taste), and he won't hit on you when he's drunk.

- *Platonic chemistry:* You meet and feel like brother and sister from the start. It's easy to be buddies because that's the soul level on which you both clicked.

The guy friendships I describe in this book assume that you've reached the just-good-friends stage after navigating one or more of the forms mentioned. Although platonic pals have the usual man-traits such as being protective and being Mr. Fix-it if he's handy, you can move your friend status from good to great by knowing a bit about his Sun sign nature. For example, trading naughty innuendos with a Gemini guy is part of the package. Flirting with a Scorpio pal sends a mixed signal that can hurt your friendship.

Astrology Basics

No two people are exactly alike, and neither are any two birth charts. Even twins born a few minutes apart have different personalities. The placement of the planets and their aspects, or angles, to each other at the time of birth can greatly affect the Sun sign personality. The earthiest Virgo will have a more spontaneous side if she has some Fire placed proximately in her chart. And the most analytical Air sign will be more emotional with Water aspects. Yet, each Sun sign personality shares some common characteristics.

In astrology, there are four elements, three qualities, and two dualities.

The *elements* are Fire, Earth, Air, and Water. An element represents the most basic characteristics of the sign. Each sign within an element will have similar traits. How those traits are expressed is modified by the quality and polarity.

- The *Fire* signs are Aries, Leo, and Sagittarius. *Action* is associated with Fire. Words such as *impulsive, outspoken, opti-*

mistic, and sometimes, *overconfident* can apply to Fire individuals. Fire sign pals are usually cheerful and upbeat. They'll come to our pity party, but they won't let us whine for long.

- The *Earth* signs are Taurus, Virgo, and Capricorn. *Caution* is associated with Earth. *Considerate, methodical, thrifty,* and *persistent* are some traits of Earth individuals. Earth sign girlfriends help us get through the rotten days with their practical advice and thoughtfulness.
- The *Air* signs are Gemini, Libra, and Aquarius. *Communication* is a key word for Air. So are *chatty, curious, sociable,* and sometimes, *gossipy.* Air sign chums are the ones we can vent to for hours on the phone. They are responsive, honest, and very clever.
- The *Water* signs are Cancer, Scorpio, and Pisces. *Emotion* is the key word for Water. *Empathetic, intuitive, caring,* and *moody* are common traits of Water signs. Water sign friends give us tea and sympathy. They offer patience, inspiration, and encouragement.

The *qualities* are Cardinal (dominant), Fixed (constant), and Mutable (flexible).

- The *Cardinal* signs are Aries, Cancer, Libra, and Capricorn. These are the *initiators* of change. They are outgoing and like to start new enterprises. Sometimes, their take-charge attitudes stir up trouble. They are also the first in line to back your latest idea and cheer your success.
- The *Fixed* signs are Taurus, Leo, Scorpio, and Aquarius. These *perfectors* can be resistant to change, preferring to stick with and refine their routines. They hold on to their beliefs, sometimes even when they are proved wrong. Their stubbornness can be exasperating. But, once these girls like you, they'll back you up no matter what.

- The *Mutable* signs are Gemini, Virgo, Sagittarius, and Pisces. These are the *adaptors* who don't get shook up when plans change. They are eager to make new friends and usually like most everyone they meet. While their tendencies to forget the clock can make them late, they also don't mind being awakened if you need to call in the middle of the night.

The *dualities* are Masculine (assertive) and Feminine (receptive).

- The *Masculine* signs are Aries, Gemini, Leo, Libra, Sagittarius, and Aquarius—the Fire and Air signs. They aren't afraid to say what they think, even if it's to verbally kick your butt.
- The *Feminine* signs are Taurus, Cancer, Virgo, Scorpio, Capricorn, and Pisces—the Earth and Water signs. These pals are introspective and usually have good intuition.

Each Sun sign is composed of one duality, one quality, and one element. For example, Virgo is the only Feminine, Mutable, Earth sign in the zodiac. Taurus, too, is Feminine and Earth. While both are receptive, thoughtful, and loyal, your Taurus friend's Fixed nature makes her naturally a little more stubborn about her point of view and less flexible about changing plans than a Virgo pal.

Venus and the Moon

In astrology, the position of Venus and the Moon indicates our instinctive emotional responses (Moon) and how we express ourselves in personal relationships (Venus). To understand your girlfriends better, it's helpful to know a little bit about these two important placements.

Venus through the signs modifies the Sun's character and influences how she deals with everyone from her mom to her best friend.

For example, even the most rational Aquarius will have a definite romantic streak if her Venus is in Pisces. Or the shyest Taurus will have a natural flirty side with Venus in Gemini. It indicates the way she gives and receives affection, forms close relationships, and demonstrates her sense of beauty and balance.

The Moon reveals her inner makeup, what she is deep down inside, and how she reacts on a gut level to people and situations. The energy of the Moon defines her sensitive, compassionate, and protective side and her need for both emotional and financial security. The most cheerful Sagittarius will have a definite moody cycle with a Cancer Moon, while a shop-till-she-drops Libra will be much more money conscious if her Moon is in thrifty Virgo. Many Internet astrology sites will produce a free natal chart that indicates the sign of Venus and the Moon at the time of birth.

Now that you have a few basics, it's time to dig deeper and peel back the layers of your Sun sign girlfriends, and learn a little about your guy pals too. Once you do, you'll understand the motivation behind some of their behaviors and how to preserve, protect, and deepen those cherished friendship bonds.

Chapter One
Aries

March 20–April 19

Element: Fire

Quality: Cardinal

Symbol: The Ram

Ruler: Mars

Birthstone: Diamond

Colors: Shades of red to orange, pastels

Flowers: Geranium, honeysuckle, sweet peas

Fragrances: Cinnamon, almond, orange, and floral musks

Soul Design

When real people fall down,
they get right back up and keep walking.
ACTRESS SARAH JESSICA PARKER (MARCH 25)

Impulsive.

Passionate.

Selfish.

She's the first sign of the zodiac and has been called everything from ballsy to bitchy. Her jets are always on high, and she is happiest when she's leading a cause, the gang, or is first in line waiting for tickets at the box office. She's also going to be the first girlfriend to rush to your side for a wild night of fun or to hug you and hand you a tissue when you're having a rotten day, as long as she feels that she's the number one friend in your life.

Your Aries best friend is ruled by Mars, the fiery, volatile, warrior planet that rules the First House of Self. Mars's energy is hot, bright, and passionate. So is she. This girl is impatient, restless, energetic, and full of life. Aries pals are not reserved. She'll push her way through a crowd and argue with anyone who says that she's cutting in line.

Ever get the feeling that she acts as if the world revolves around her? You're right. Hers does. Reincarnation tells us that Aries is the baby of the Universe. In the First House of Self, the soul begins its journey around the zodiac wheel. Her young soul is preoccupied with its personal world, just as a real baby is preoccupied with its own fingers and toes. She needs to feel bonded to you, as a baby needs to bond with a parent. Remember that. Making casual friends with an Aries is easy. She loves to meet new people and usually will take the lead in introducing herself. Keeping her close requires that you understand that, although she can be hot headed and a little pushy, inside she's as vulnerable as the toddler who needs constant love and support.

She can be nonstop talkative like Gemini and Sagittarius. Where Gemini chats are filled with questions about you, and Sagittarius conversations are sprinkled with philosophical sidebars, your Aries pal's dialogues are usually about herself. *First* is one of the key words with Aries. Show your interest in her by letting her talk first. She'll try to listen politely when it's your turn. What's more likely is that she'll probably interrupt to interject an anecdote about her life. This isn't as selfish as conventional astrology tells us. It's her way of proving to you that she understands and connects with you. Whether it's men, family, career, movie stars, or even food, this girl needs to constantly reassure herself that you two have something in common.

Aries is *Masculine Cardinal Fire*. As a *Cardinal* sign she wants to initiate action or lead the way for others. Being *Masculine* (assertive) with her *Fire* nature ruled by Mars makes it hard for her to listen, plan ahead, or wait for results. As when she first learned to walk, an Aries pal has to take her own emotional falls. When she does fall, telling her that you think she was brave to face a problem outright, or to march into the boss's office to ask for a raise, will make her smile. *Praise* is another Aries key word.

Her astrological symbol, the Ram, is a sure-footed creature that bounds over the hillsides without a moment's hesitation. A Ram will run headlong into an enemy without thinking to protect its territory. An Aries chum does the same. She rarely looks before she leaps and is always ready to take a stand against a perceived enemy or injustice. This chum is one of the best champions of the underdog in the zodiac. She'll fight for you the same way. While she hopes that you will fight for her, she has the unique perspective of understanding that not everyone is as strong willed as she, and she will be as appreciative of your emotional support even if you aren't the type to wade into the war with her.

This girlfriend doesn't need a pack of admirers. She's independent and can amuse herself with a variety of activities, from reading to sports. She's more likely to have a handful of special and different buddies instead of one group that she hangs with all the time. She's almost always in motion. To be more than casual chums you'll need to keep up. If you're the shy type who likes to stay in the background, you might think she's too much to hang around with on a permanent basis. You could also have the time of your life, because her fun-loving approach to life ensures you few dull moments.

As are the other Fire signs, she's full of advice. But, unlike Leo, who feels a certain responsibility to help, or Sagittarius, who can see both sides of the issue, Ms. Aries will spout all sorts of ways to fix your problems without bothering to get the facts. This girl will go so far as to volunteer to confront the issue for you. She's eager to tell off your enemies or a nasty bill collector. Your Aries pal will not hesitate to help you with a problem, offer advice, or even take control. However, she'll seldom take your advice when she's in trouble. Exasperating? You bet. She'll tell you that she's up to her ears in alligators. No matter how on target your advice is, she'll most likely reject it. Her impulsive need to jump into the fracas without a plan often lands her in trouble.

Your Aries friend might battle for the environment, women's rights, or a charitable organization. More likely, she'll focus on a personal battle. She might decide that you should lose weight, quit biting your nails, or give up some other unhealthy habit. She's the zodiac's warrior princess who needs to fight for a cause, and her usual causes are the people she loves.

An Aries girlfriend of mine was married and divorced very young and raised four children alone. She suffered a violent spouse and the loss of a child. Later she added three stepchildren to her family, and anyone else who needed a temporary place to crash. For decades her life seemed like a magnet for adversity. A softer person would have cracked, but she refused to give up. She was on a survival mission. She felt that she had to fight for her children, then her stepchildren, and now her parents and in-laws as they age. She's the one who bucks the system, argues with the doctors, and tracks down the best care. Although she's in her sixties, her daily schedule might exhaust a Gemini. She seems as tireless and energetic as ever. It's her basic instinct. An Aries woman doesn't do laid-back.

She's competitive. This Aries trait is a dual-edged sword. Her motivation and courage to accomplish whatever she tries can get skewed into a perpetual contest. Most of the time, she'll be eager to see you succeed and will be your greatest supporter. She'll brag about you to the rest of her friends and be almost as proud of your accomplishments as she is her own. Always brag about her too, because her competitive spirit arises from her inner need to have your admiration. Bragging about her in front of her is best. It fuels her need to feel important, and she thrives on encouragement. It reassures her that she's doing well and that you're proud and happy to be her friend.

The worst thing you can do to an Aries is criticize her. Her self-confidence is as vulnerable as the false bravado of a small child. She may be the hardest-driving career woman you know, or the girl with a string of guys fighting for her cell number, but you can burst her bubble with an offhand comment. Her hair looks drab. Her outfit is outdated. Outwardly, she may get pissed and fire off a comeback. Inside, she'll be crushed. Do it too often and she'll disappear. If you need to call her attention to an issue, do it honestly and gently. Start with praise, then suggest the change.

That churning Martian energy sometimes makes her touchy and irritable. Usually, it's when she's overexerted herself. Rams can go from energetic to hyperactive in a heartbeat. Don't try to calm her down. You can't. Suggesting a relaxed evening that would soothe a Taurus, Cancer, or Pisces won't work. Instead, offer to go for a walk with her, take her for a drive, or to the gym or dancing. She needs action to unwind. Otherwise, her overamped energy will turn into a highly charged flow of snippy remarks that could put the sharpest-tongued Scorpio to shame.

Mostly, she's full of life and eager to please. She may try to tell you what to do, but she will respect the fact that you want to do things your way. Your Aries girlfriend is part Joan of Arc, part Lady Godiva, and part Orphan Annie. It's an interesting mix. What you see is what you get with her. If you want a pal who is straightforward, who never loses her childlike interest in life, and who will help you to fight any battle, she's your girl.

Groove Meter

I have a big, flamboyant, open personality. . . .
ACTRESS KATE HUDSON (APRIL 19)

A playful Aries pal is always ready for fun. She likes to be where the action is, and like Gemini and Sagittarius, she's one girl who will drop everything for a good time. The difference is that most times she'll call you first with news of anything from the hot Internet deal for a girls-only cruise to a pizza and sleepover at her place.

All Fire signs need to keep busy, and easily bored Aries most of all. If you want to stay high on her list of fun friends, you'll need to act as spontaneously as she does at least part of the time. She'll understand if you aren't always ready or willing to change plans at the last minute to accommodate her newest adventure. But, turn her down too many times and she'll quit asking. Not because she doesn't like you anymore. This girl simply doesn't have the patience, or interest, to keep begging you to join the fun. The good news with your Aries pal is that even if you do lose touch, if you call to catch up or to invite her out, she'll be eager to renew the friendship. Her childlike inner spirit works that way. Time or distance doesn't mean much to her, and once you're her friend, you're always a friend.

She has a built-in need to have the last word. It's that Martian competitive streak. Although it can be irksome, try to think of it as a harmless quirk. Whether you're on email or the phone, if you say, "So long," she'll say, "Buh-bye." You say, "Okay." She responds with "Right." What do you do? Ignore her. She's in toddler mode. If you call her on it, she'll laugh, but it's unlikely she'll change.

Most Aries women are health conscious, which makes her a great gym buddy. She'll encourage you to stick with the program or, more likely, turn it into a competition to see which of you reaches your goal first. Be prepared to work your butt off. She will. She'll also push you as hard as she pushes herself, to ensure that you succeed too.

Need to plan a last-minute party? Call her. Like Cancer and Sagittarius, she'll love to help you pull it together, and she'll do a great job. She doesn't mind running all over town with you to pick up the food or decorations. She'll also get the fun started by making sure everyone gets introduced or initiating an ice-breaker game.

All Fire signs love a bash, and if the party's for her she'll adore being the guest of honor. Whereas Leo likes the spotlight because she likes being the center of attention, your Aries pal seeks attention because it's an acknowledgment of her importance in your life. While she does like to be surprised, if you really want to thrill her, tell her what you are planning. Letting her choose the decorations or some food items or remind you not to forget to invite someone really makes her feel special.

This girlfriend likes gifts that give her an experience as much or more than tangible presents. She will love tickets to a play, a concert, or a sporting event. Buy her a gift certificate for a golf or flying lesson. She loves to read, but her attention span isn't as long as those of some other signs, so buy her shorter books, such as action-packed thrillers or romance novels that engage her amorous side.

If she's getting married, she'll love a time-saving appliance for the kitchen. Maybe a juicer that appeals to both her need for speed and her quest for health. Something sexy and drop-dead red for her boudoir will appeal to her passionate nature.

Whether she's nineteen or ninety, your Aries girlfriend is a go-getter who needs plenty of excitement in her life. She's continually looking for something new and interesting to do, and you can count on her to always be ready to rock and roll.

Speed Bumps

Sometimes it's worse to win a fight than to lose.
AMERICAN JAZZ SINGER BILLIE HOLLIDAY (APRIL 7)

Your Aries pal doesn't always stop to think about how her actions will affect you. As a Cardinal sign, along with sisters Cancer, Libra, and Capricorn, an Aries likes to lead. What's better than calling all the shots? Compound this with her first time on the zodiac soul trip, and the result is an eager, excitable woman who has a definite selfish streak.

She's full of contradictions. Sincere and outspoken, an Aries friend will do anything in her power to help you if you need her. She also won't hesitate to tell you that she doesn't like one of your other friends or that your latest haircut looks like it was chewed by a lawnmower. Is this a double standard from earlier, where I told you that her feelings are easily wounded? You bet. In her view, she's trying to be helpful. If you wince under the weight of her blunt observations, she'll be quick to apologize, but that won't stop her from being as outspoken the next time. Look at the bright side. Not many girlfriends will give you as honest an opinion. When you need to hear the truth, your Aries pal is one you can count on to tell it, even if it hurts.

Whether it's a night out with the girls or a weekend road trip, the lady Ram might try to take the initiative to plan the occasion even if you've already made arrangements. At the least she'll have a few ideas on how to make the trip or evening more exciting. If you say, "Thanks, but no thanks," to her suggestions, she can get pushy. Plus, she won't hesitate to say, "I told you so," should a glitch arise in your plan. In fact, she'll take unabashed glee in pointing it out. Annoying? Oh, yes. Remember that she's operating from her childlike need to feel important. Instead of arguing, tell her that next time you'll get her opinion first. Whether you do or not, you'll satisfy and shut her up for the moment.

Her temper is legendary. Think of Rosie O'Donnell's very public feud with Gemini Donald Trump. Whether you think she was right or wrong, Rosie didn't miss a heartbeat in telling the world what she thought of his perceived manipulation and "ownership" of the Miss America contest. With full-scale Aries fire and brimstone, she went ballistic when Trump shot back with his own sarcastic—and typically Gemini—barbs, and the feud quickly escalated into a lengthy, primetime war. In classic Aries style, Rosie shot from the lip without thinking how her behavior would affect anyone else. Her opinion was all that mattered to her, damn the consequences.

Luckily, your chum will hardly be as bratty as Rosie. Usually an Aries girl erupts like a volcano, then quiets as fast. Think of the two-year-old's temper tantrum. Once it's over, it's forgotten. Every Ram explodes a little now and then. She needs to blow off her Martian energy. In fact, it's emotionally healthy for her. Bottle it up, and this girl can stir up lots of trouble to keep herself from being bored. She may yell or smash a dish or two. Then she feels better, cheerfully cleans up the mess, and moves to the next thing on her agenda. You should be on alert if she gets quiet. That's when she's really hurt or angry, and when she's either moving in for the kill or moving out of your life. It takes a lot to hurt an Aries that badly, and if you do, you'll most likely deserve to have her tap dance on your head.

Even if you're her best friend in the Universe, her selfish side can sometimes make you want to scream. You may have just held her head through the hangover from hell, listened to her vent for hours about her stupid boss, or bought her lunch because she was short on cash. Yet, she won't always make time for you. If you're going to make it work, you'll need to remember it's the baby thing and try to be patient.

She truly lives in her own world, more so than other signs. Pisces may seem out of it, but Pisces retreats from the world. Aries flies headlong into it, then tries to mold it to fit her needs, sometimes without regard to anything or anyone else.

Romance Rating

*Love is a fire. But, whether it's going to warm
your hearth or burn down your house, you can never tell.*
CLASSIC MOVIE STAR JOAN CRAWFORD (MARCH 23)

Love is the ultimate competition for your Aries pal, which is why she may have lots of man trouble. The same way she likes to lead the gang, she likes to rule her relationships. This is because her soul needs a challenge, and pushing for limits is one way to get it. Unfortunately, this sets the stage for a series of broken love bonds.

She's definitely not a fluttering, helpless female. If she acts that way, you can bet she's laying a trap for some unsuspecting guy. Although she loves romance, it's the thrill of the chase combined with a continual emotional fencing contest to see who's boss that keeps her interested. Unlike Leo, whose self-confidence issues are at the root of her bossy side, Aries' ego is driven by the need to meet a man on equal terms. She appreciates a man who's as strong as she is and wants him to stand up to her.

Too many times, she ends up with a guy she can boss around but doesn't respect, or worse, a problem child who expects her to save him. Because she needs a crusade, for awhile she will make him her cause. The downside is that the worse the guy acts, the more she might try to hang on and change him. The results can be disastrous.

She's one of the most jealous girls in the zodiac. She's as possessive as any Water sign, but not because she's insecure. She wants to be number one. If he has too many nights out with the boys, she'll rebel in her volatile style. I've never known an Aries woman with a smooth-sailing love life. She's like a speedboat. The choppier the waves, the more exciting the ride.

When she gets hurt, you and everyone else will know. She's neither stoic nor shy about venting her feelings or above plotting revenge on the man who made her cry. Rush to her. Under the rage is a little soul that crumbles when she's wounded. She'll give you a blow-by-blow description of every detail of the fight, and it might take hours for her to calm down. When she's in a full-throttle rant, be prepared to listen. She doesn't want solutions. She needs to get the anger out and to know that you are unconditionally on her side.

Once the clouds clear, you can offer advice. As I said earlier, she probably won't take it, but she'll appreciate your input. If she makes up with the guy, she'll act as though nothing happened in the first place. A secret about this feisty girl is that she's not above picking a fight with her man if life runs a little too smoothly. Smooth equals boring to an Aries, and she'd rather stir up turmoil than be one-half of your average couple.

If your heart is broken, she'll make it her mission to cheer you up. She'll be happy to tell off your jerky boyfriend if it makes you feel better. If he's done something really terrible, like cheating, she might tell him off even if you don't want her to. It's her crusader side dispensing justice.

Be warned. She'll compete with you for male attention. This can range from minor flirting to a race to see who snags a new hottie first. While every sign can vie for male attention and every friendship needs ground rules on man-spotting behavior, I'm sorry to say that Ms. Aries might not always uphold her end of the bargain. So if you're both on the prowl at the same time, and have the same taste in men, look your best—and wear your track shoes.

Bitch Factor

I know I've been a perfect bitch.
But I couldn't help myself.
CLASSIC MOVIE STAR BETTE DAVIS (APRIL 5)

Aries bad behaviors range from appallingly selfish to balls-out ruth-less. Unevolved Rams are arrogant and self-absorbed. Whether it's nonstop chatter to get all the attention at lunch or blatantly making a pass at your man, these bad girls have to win at all costs.

Self-serving Samantha is first on the list. Although relatively harmless, on a soul level she's the poster girl for selfish behavior. Her favorite word is *I*. "I decided for the group." "I want." "I need." "I'm taking over." She'll fire off a hurtful remark, then be genuinely shocked when you get angry. That's because she's as clueless as they come.

Samantha is one of the biggest gossips in the Universe. Never con-fide anything to her unless you're okay with having it broadcast around the office or your hometown faster than CNN can air the latest-breaking story. Spreading rumors or embellishing a hot issue is one way she tries to make herself look important. It won't matter if you are her best friend, mom, sister, or latest lover; no one is immune to her flapping lips.

Fortunately, she is so transparent that you won't have any trouble spotting her. She usually sinks herself by shooting off her big mouth once too often.

Next is the Troublemaker. She has all the negative qualities of Samantha, but she's half an I.Q. point smarter. At first, she might seem like a quiet Ram—thoughtful, even introspective. Truth is she has more neuroses than the worst anxiety-ridden Gemini. She'll try to cause a rift within your inner circle because she wants all your atten-tion. If she can't have it, she'll try to usurp your place in the group by gossiping to stir up trouble. It gets her the attention she craves and is designed to make you look like the bad girl.

She'll pull this trick at work if she's competing with you for a pro-motion, wants your job, or seeks to gain favor with the boss. No one in the Universe is as important or as smart as she is, so she thinks.

At work, the Troublemaker comes on like an eager team player. Soon, she'll start making suggestions. How she can do it better. How you need help. She will make them to you, to your coworkers, and to the boss. If you confront her, she's likely to demand a meeting on the pretext of working out any misunderstandings. The misunderstanding will be if you fall for her backstabbing behavior. She doesn't want to work anything out. She wants to prove to the boss that she is better than you and everyone else in the office. At her worst, she won't hesitate to sabotage a project to make you look bad.

The remedy? Kick this one's ass to the curb and don't be coy about it. She'll yelp that you hurt her feelings, but since her attention span is shorter than her miniskirt, by the time the bruises heal she'll have found new victims to torment.

Last, and lowest on the awful-Aries list, is Slutty Sue. This one thinks she oozes sex appeal and frequently dresses like a hooker and acts like a nympho. She won't hesitate to put the make on any man, including yours, any time or place and invite you along for the ride or to watch. Even if she's well past prime time, her attention-getting antics could make the most obnoxious Leo look like a wall-flower. Old Sue will still wear a miniskirt (with tights to hide her varicose-veined legs), a clingy sweater, and shoulder-length dyed-any-color hair. From behind she might appear relatively young. Turn her around and you'll find yourself staring into a face that resembles the taxidermied dead mother in *Psycho*.

Slutty Sue is terminally horny. She's a total pleasure seeker, and there are no rules in her world. Whoever gets laid first wins. There's no way you can form a bond with this one, even if you are into group sex, are an exhibitionist yourself, or like to lap dance on the nearest stranger. If you have two partners, Sue will have five, take pictures, and proudly broadcast them on the Internet.

Fortunately, as with other Fire sign bimbos, subtly isn't an issue, and Sue's easy to spot because of her self-important attitude and zero finesse. Walk away. Silence is deadly to an Aries. She doesn't know how to deal with it because she feeds on pushing your buttons. If you switch off, you cut her fuel supply, and she'll burn up and out.

Bondability

Sister of the soul: Sagittarius, Gemini
Inner circle: Aries, Taurus, Leo, Aquarius
Party pal: Libra, Pisces
Casual chum: Cancer, Virgo, Scorpio, Capricorn
Famous Aries friendship: Sarah Jessica Parker and Cynthia Nixon
(also an Aries)

♈

Venus in Aries

Aries is a demonstrative sign, and Venus here gives even the shyest Virgo or reserved Scorpio a brash, in-your-face edge. Fiery Mars ignites Venus's passion while overpowering her more subtle traits. It sharpens her competitiveness and adds an impatient edge to the most patient of signs. Aries Venus likes to have the upper hand, whether it's in romance or in friendship, and gives a vocal, passionate aspect to any sign.

She's more independent, prone to casual flirting, and has a definite jealous streak. She also has the tendency to fall in love at first sight, no matter how reserved her Sun sign nature might be. She might have lots of platonic (or bed buddy) guy friendships.

Just as an Aries Sun, Venus in Aries prefers to be a trendsetter. Depending on her age, she might have been the first in your group to iron her hair or to try Botox. This placement gives a cutting-edge sense to her fashion style, and she'll love to make a statement. Venus in Aries is impulsive and often will give an "I have to have that, now!" edge to the Sun sign personality.

Even if she's a conservative Capricorn, chances are that she'll love bold red lipsticks and have a few vibrantly colored sweaters or dresses. A Venus Aries beauty ritual includes the latest moisturizers and hydrating body lotions. A pal with this placement often buys every new beauty product that comes out, but she gets bored with them just as fast. She's likely to have a stash of barely used cosmetics and skin care items piled beneath the bathroom vanity.

Moon in Aries

The rash Aries Moon bestows an impulsive, reckless emotional nature to any Sun sign. An Aries Moon is spontaneous and quick thinking. This girlfriend takes charge in an emotional crisis and is able to resolve the most difficult issues. She rarely passes up an opportunity, whether it's cheerfully plunging into a new hobby, romance, or friendship or sizing up the best way to get a promotion at work.

This girlfriend's emotional structure is to leap first and not think about the consequences at all. You can call her the original "oops" girl, because that will be about the extent of her angst if something she's tried doesn't work out. Try to warn her about her latest crazy scheme or dangerous liaison and her eyes will glaze over. This Moon can push the most reclusive Cancer into ballsy adventures like impulsively booking an insanely expensive vacation or plastering half-naked pictures of herself on the Internet.

An Aries Moon girlfriend has a quick temper and independent nature. Even if she's a Scorpio who controls her outward emotional reactions, you can see a momentary flash of anger in her eyes when she's upset. In a Fire Sun sign, temper tantrums can become a way of life! The good news is that this Moon sign rarely holds a grudge. She's one of the most forgiving pals in the zodiac.

Your Aries Guy Pal

He comes in two types—a macho man who lives life in the fast lane or a macho man who likes to quietly pull the strings behind the scenes. An Aries guy is always on a personal quest to make his mark on the world. Whether it's climbing the corporate ladder or winning the office bowling tournament, he needs to feel he's a cut above the herd.

An Aries man needs freedom in his friendship. You may not see him for weeks, then he'll suddenly show up or call and ask if you want to get a beer or go to the game.

If you're really tight, he's likely to confess when his relationship hits a snag or he gets dumped because he wants your sympathy. Give it to him and pump his ego by listing all his virtues. This pal doesn't have a fragile ego, so it won't take much to get him back on track.

Don't expect too much advice should your love life hit the rocks. He's usually not the type who can handle heavy-duty emotions.

He is great to rely on when you need some hard body work done. Call him when you're moving, or if you want to rearrange the furniture. He'll love to go car shopping with you. However, he's into flash, speed, and showing off, so don't expect him to love the gas-efficient money savers. He's also a pal to take to a party when you don't want to go solo. Aries guys usually love to dance and have no trouble mixing with strangers. He probably won't stick by your side all evening because he's off collecting phone numbers.

Whether he's quiet or outrageous, in his heart, every Aries man thinks he's an outlaw. Treat him as if you believe it, be enthusiastic and give him space, and he'll be your hero and a devoted buddy.

Chapter Two
Taurus

April 20–May 20
Element: Earth
Quality: Fixed
Symbol: The Bull
Ruler: Venus
Birthstone: Emerald
Colors: Blue, brown, copper tones, yellows, and deep reds
Flowers: Poppy, violet, daisy
Fragrances: Vanilla musk, woodsy florals, moss, and lime

Soul Design

If you obey all the rules, you'll miss all the fun.
CLASSIC MOVIE STAR KATHARINE HEPBURN (MAY 12)

Gentle.

Reliable.

Stubborn.

Ruled by Venus, the goddess of love and beauty, your Taurus girl-friend definitely appreciates the finer things in life. Yes, she's more laid-back than party hardy. But, she's definitely not a totally lazy, stingy, or terminally stubborn woman.

This girl is *Feminine Fixed Earth*. All Fixed signs have specific beliefs. All Earth signs need some measure of stability. Your Taurus friend's stubborn rep doesn't stem so much from the fact that she likes to have everything her way, as sister Leo does. Taurus doesn't like change. Whether it's coffee every Thursday or a Saturday morning mall crawl, if you have a standing girlfriend date, try your best to stick to the routine. Your cat's sick or you've broken a leg are acceptable excuses; cleaning your room or dropping her because your latest squeeze dropped by aren't.

Unlike Air signs that get off on not knowing what's going to happen next, or Fire signs that thrive on new adventures, a Taurus pal is a creature of habit. Routines make her feel comfortable and secure.

So do tangible things. Her soul lives in the Second House of Possessions, Values, and Money, and the key word in this crib changes from *I* to *mine*. As does sister Scorpio, Taurus has trust issues. Scorpio is cautious about trusting people with her deep emotions. Taurus trusts what she owns. A home, a bank account, things that last, such as good furniture and art, all make this girl feel safe. She also trusts proven relationships, like a close-knit circle of old friends.

Taurus is one of the girls who make forever friends, starting in grade school. A Taurus relative of mine once told me that the happiest time in her life was when she and her first husband had moved back to their hometown and, eventually, several of her childhood friends and their families moved into the same neighborhood. They had weekly potlucks, shared babysitting duty, and often vacationed together. This girlfriend thrives in an extended family situation where there are few surprises.

Of course, this doesn't mean that if you're a new pal that she won't grow to like you just as much. But, it's helpful to understand how she views her relationships and what she expects from them. She would rather make quality relationships with chums on whom she can depend than be the most popular girl at the ball. Proving that you are dependable by returning her phone calls, keeping your word, and not flaking out on her too many times will help to get you admitted to her inner circle. Her emotional bonds grow slowly, like a tree putting down roots, and they go as deep.

Some astrology tomes call her boring. That's wrong. Libra inherited Venus's social traits. Taurus values Venus's love of simplicity. She appreciates consistency and serenity. Want to spend a day in the park or a long weekend at the beach sleeping, eating, and soaking up the sun? This is the girlfriend to call. She knows how to relax and can help you to see both the power and the pleasure in taking time to enjoy life in today's frantic world.

Your Taurus best friend has a personal set of criteria by which she measures everyone. It's her Venus-ruled discrimination. She's not easily influenced by what others think. Where Libra, the other Venus-ruled sign, can more easily see both sides of a situation, a Taurus woman's Fixed nature makes her rely upon her own opinions, whether she's right or wrong. This can be a pain when you're trying to argue your case. You might get her to compromise because she really is peace loving at heart. As with every other Fixed sign, you'll rarely get her to change her mind when she thinks she's right.

The quote by Katharine Hepburn makes it sound as if your Taurus chum is a rebel. Not so. She obeys the rules, when they make sense to her. If she thinks it's unfair, unwarranted, or plain stupid, she'll either try to change it or ignore it and do it her way—as Ms. Hepburn did when she began appearing in public dressed in slacks. Early Hollywood's standard portrayal of women needing rescuing didn't appeal to her. Neither did the idea of a movie heroine tramping through the underbrush in low-cut dress and heels. It was stupid.

Real women didn't do that; neither did they always need to be saved by men. Hepburn pushed it a step farther by being photographed in men's trousers in real life. Is that stubborn? Maybe. But, a Taurus woman is stubborn with a purpose rather than simply being arbitrary.

Her zodiac symbol of the Bull is often associated with words such as *bull-headed,* or *bullish,* and suggests a bad temper. Yes, she can be fierce when she's pushed. But you have to push hard to ruffle her patient nature. Flash tempers belong to the Fire signs and touchy feelings to Water babies. The Bull rarely charges unless she's provoked or threatened. If you are in the vicinity when she does explode, duck and don't try to calm her down. The best thing to do is leave her alone until she cools down, which can take hours or days. If you've caused the rift, immediately apologize, and make sure that it's genuine. She'll forgive you. She won't forget. You shouldn't either. Once you know what pushes her anger button, if you want to keep her close, don't go there again. You can't tease this girlfriend. Good-natured kidding is okay, but she's not into trading wisecracks like you can do with your Gemini or Sagittarius buddies.

Your Taurus chum is a Feminine sign and is often referred to as the sensualist of the zodiac. Her sensual side goes much deeper than the sexual reference. Taste, texture, color, fragrance, and anything that is visually beautiful attracts and affects her. Invite her to go antique shopping. She's one girl who appreciates both the history and value of handcrafted objects. Usually, she'll be the girlfriend who actually uses her grandmother's china instead of keeping it tucked away in a cabinet.

Her reputation as one of the luxury lovers of the zodiac is not quite right. Capricorn loves luxury. Taurus loves comfort. If comfort comes with a large price tag, she'll pay it. She might have dozens of pairs of shoes, an expensive art collection, or the latest sound system. She's not, however, prone to breaking her budget to prove she can have the best, as Libra or Leo is. Neither is she as thrifty as Virgo about going without. Within your Taurus pal, Venus's eye for comfort and style blends near-perfectly with the Bull's earthy practicality. The result is a girl who can find the most heavenly stuff at value prices. This is because she has the patience and determination to shop all day, or all week, until she finds both quality and a bargain. This is the girl-friend to take when you're on a mission to find that one, special item *and* stay within your budget.

She's sentimental. This chum, along with Cancer, might still have her favorite teddy bear, or a pillow she's made that's stuffed with her baby blanket. It's said that when Taurus Barbra Streisand was regularly on tour she traveled with personal items such as throw pillows and framed family pictures, and had vases of flowers and other homey touches added to her hotel suites. This is a typical Taurus trait and explains why your pal might refuse to travel without her favorite pillow or cozy comforter. She feels more secure with a few well-loved objects nearby.

She may not seem overtly emotional, but even the smallest kindness will touch her. Giving her an unexpected fun gift or silly card to let her know you appreciate her will keep you near and dear. Loyalty and faithfulness are important to this pal. She's devoted, caring, and one of the girlfriends you can call at any hour for help. She may never call you at 2 A.M. because she prefers to work out her problems alone. If she does ask for help, you can bet that she's in dire need. Either way, knowing that you are there if she needs you is what counts.

A Taurus women isn't too concerned with grabbing all the attention. If she's a public figure, being in the spotlight is a means to an end. She'll use her fame to fight for a cause, but quietly, by putting her money where her mouth is and working behind the scenes. I have a great friend who is the heart and soul of several local women's groups. She organizes conferences, is the executive director of a nonprofit organization, and is the go-to person for everything from budget control to the luncheon menus. Yet, you would never know it unless someone told you. She's working to help people, not to collect personal kudos.

She wants the best for herself, and she's willing to work hard to achieve it; with her naturally laid-back nature, she'll know a few shortcuts. It's said that if you want to get a lot done in a short time, take it to a busy person. A contradiction to this cliché is to take it to a lazy person—laziness, not necessity, might be the mother of invention. Your Taurus chum loves her downtime, and she's a whiz at finding the least effortful way of doing an otherwise labor-intensive chore, both at home and at the office. Next time you're faced with a multitasking nightmare, ask for her advice. She'll always have a couple of timesaving and obvious suggestions that help to take the pressure off. She's probably the one sign in the zodiac that can out-organize a Virgo when she's on a roll. That's because she has none of Virgo's self-inflicted nervous tension and is able to virtually shut out everything around her to focus on the task at hand.

Tenacious, sometimes willful, and usually more reserved than reckless, your Taurus BFF is into quality, not quantity. She's not impressed by flash and dash or here-today-gone-tomorrow friendships. That's why it might take you a little longer to get into her best buddies group, but once there, you can count on this girlfriend bond to stand the test of time.

Groove Meter

I'm part extrovert, part wallflower.
ACTRESS CATE BLANCHETT (MAY 14)

Your Taurus girlfriend can be ballsy and outgoing one night and totally shy the next. Her intensity level works the same way. If you charted her energy output, it would look like a spiky graph. She has outbursts of liveliness, then retreats to recharge her batteries.

Whether you're dancing to the beat of the latest rock band or hanging out at the sports bar with a group of coed chums, the key to partying with a Taurus is that she is surrounded by her friends. This is when you're most likely to see your average Taurus pal's extroverted side. A lady Bull can get as rowdy as the wildest Leo and be so funny that she keeps everyone in stitches. Think of comedienne Carol Burnett and megastar Shirley MacLaine.

Just as she prefers familiar faces, she'll have a few favorite places that she likes to go. While she won't hesitate to try any new place that you might suggest, the unknown can make her nervous. When she's unsure of herself, the wallflower appears. She's not a girl who will rush headlong into an unfamiliar social situation. Take her to a party where she doesn't know anyone and soon she'll be in the quietest corner of the room sipping her drink and watching the action. Air and Fire signs look on the unknown as an adventure. Earth and Water signs relax around people and places they know.

Your Taurus girlfriend approaches fun as she does everything else, leisurely. Her Venus-ruled soul knows the value of time spent in appreciation of a nature hike or frequent stops on a road trip to take in the views. Any outdoor event, from a backyard bash to a pickup Frisbee game in the park to a weekend cruise appeals to her. If you feel like playing hooky on occasion, she's the perfect pal to call in sick with and head out of town for a day trip, or to the nearest spa for some serious pampering.

She's generous. She'll buy you the nicest gifts she can afford, bring more than her share of snacks to a party, and won't keep score on who bought the last hamburger.

When she's in the mood, she's one chum who can party everyone else under the table. But you can trust her to be the designated driver too. She'll take seriously her responsibility to see that everyone gets home safely.

A Taurus pal is good-natured enough to let herself be taken advantage of sometimes. She won't say anything, but she will notice that she's doing more than her share. If you want to stay high on her BFF list, don't take her for granted.

Most Taurus women like sports. She's great to take along to anything from a pro baseball game to a girls-against-the-guys bowling tournament. She's one pal who'll try the indoor climbing wall with you or head down the Colorado on a river-rafting trip.

It's hard to surprise a Taurus girlfriend. If it's close to her birthday, she'll drop hints or try to pry details out of your mutual pals. Her behavior is based on insecurity. She's hoping that you haven't forgotten her. She can get pretty cagey in trying to discover what you're planning, so if you truly want to surprise her, lie. Tell her your folks are planning a family reunion or anything else that makes her think she's not getting a party. Hand her a card a couple of days early to reinforce the charade.

Money is always a good gift for a Taurus—cash for the under-thirty crowd and gift cards for your older pals. She'll like a CD, as she usually appreciates all types of music, from country to classical. Clothing is great as long as it's soft to the touch. If you buy her a sweater, gloves, or anything that goes next to her skin, make sure it feels silky, cozy, or luxurious. Most Taurus pals have some sort of collection. Whether it's seashells or antique jewelry, she'll love it if you take the time to pick out something special to add. She'll like gift certificates to her favorite restaurant, even if it's a fast-food chain.

Bridal gifts should be selected from the registry, as she usually has a definite style in mind for her home. As her tastes run to the expensive, she'll appreciate acquiring her china, crystal, and state-of-the-art cookware as gifts.

A Taurus girlfriend is down to earth, unpretentious, and loyal, and you won't have to worry whether she likes you one minute and will drop you for another pal the next.

Speed Bumps

If I'm too strong for some people,
that's their problem.
ACTRESS GLENDA JACKSON (MAY 9)

Let's get it over with. Yes, your Taurus girlfriend is always right. Or so she'll say, time and time again. Her need to cling to her belief or judgment or way of doing things isn't based on ego, like a Leo, or intellect like Aquarius, or control like Scorpio, the other Fixed signs. She's Fixed Earth, and just as it takes an earthquake to shake up the ground, sometimes it takes a metaphorical one to make a Taurus change her mind. That's part of the explanation.

The rest of the story is that, for all of the outer strength and determination she shows to the world, she can be full of anxiety and insecurity about any type of change. Her Second House soul is like the five-year-old who's anxious about the first day of kindergarten or the older toddler who refuses to share her toys. She will cling to her mother until gently pushed toward the teacher or never play with the toy unless someone else picks it up; then she'll wail, "That's mine!"

It's the same with her life in general. She can be so fearful of making a move that she'll settle for the status quo. It's a large part of the reason that she has the reputation for being stubborn. It explains why she may have a storage unit filled with those childhood toys or boxes of collectibles that she'll never dust off and display. Earlier I said that she trusts what she owns. This includes her belief system and routines. While you're shaking your head or your fist at her, remembering this fact will help you keep your cool.

The flip side is that, if you can prove that another way works better, she'll immediately (and I mean in a heartbeat) change her mind. Once she does, she'll own whatever it is that you had to push, prod, and threaten her to try. No sweat. It's a snap. You should be proud of yourself for having enough patience or fortitude to keep at it. Feed her the facts, show her examples, and argue if you have to, but sooner or later you can break through her fear.

She's possessive. Taurus girlfriends collect people as well as objects. If you're her friend, in a very real sense you belong to her. Not the Gemini you run around with when you want to shake things up a little, or the Capricorn when you're in the mood to shop for designer handbags. This can really irritate you if you're Fire or Air and used to having a lot of casual pals. But, to the Bull, you are *her* friend. She won't stamp her foot and demand attention, as a Fire chum would, or get in a snit, as your Water pal will. She simply won't understand why you need anyone but her and your inner circle of chums to hang with. The easiest way to handle this situation is to get the rules straight at the beginning of your friendship. Talk about your casual pals or introduce her to them. And don't forget the standing date. Whether it's a weekly movie night, or daily text exchange to keep in touch, as long as you check with her on a regular basis, she'll feel okay.

She can hold a grudge and bitch about it until your ears burn. Taurus may be the sign of the Bull, but these girlfriends have memories like elephants. A phony friend spread gossip about her. A traitor at work tried to steal her job. A traitor in her crew tried to steal her man. The fact that any of these incidents happened any time from yesterday to years ago won't mean anything when she's on a tirade. Telling her to forget or get over it never works. Empathizing and agreeing helps her to settle down. She understands her behavior isn't logical or rational. Time usually lessens this angst, but even years later she might occasionally vent.

As do her roots of love and friendship, your Taurus chum's anger grows slowly and deep.

Romance Rating

I can't believe that people got so upset
at the sight of a single breast.
SINGER JANET JACKSON (MAY 16)

For all her Venusian sensuality and sensitivity, the lady Bull is usually a realist. She's one of those rare people who can see her man's faults and decide whether or not she can live with them before she commits to the relationship. Taurus wants a love that she can depend on. Unlike Libra, the other Venus-ruled sign, Ms. Taurus won't try to change him. She'll carefully try to pick the right one from the start, according, of course, to her perfect-man list of criteria. In that regard she can be barely less critical than Virgo. She doesn't mind waiting for the right man. This is the good news.

The bad news is that her greatest danger is similar to Leo's, in that while she searches for Mr. Right, she can get temporarily swept off her feet by a bad boy with a pretty face. Normally, she has great people instincts, but she'll push them aside if she's dazzled by a seductive charmer. It's one of the rare times that she can be fooled, and it might take a huge heartbreak before she learns that a winning smile and handsome features don't equal decency.

Another unfortunate factor is that her fear of change colors her love nature, which can make her clingy. It can be as tough for her to let go of a bad relationship as it is for a sister Water sign. Remember the tree. Her roots are the time and emotion she's put into the relationship. It's not easy for her to dig up her feelings and transplant them somewhere else. If you offer sympathy and your opinion, she'll listen and value it. As with every Fixed sign, she won't make a move until she's ready. Fortunately, when she finally extricates herself from the loser boyfriend or unhappy marriage, she'll learn from her mistakes and rarely make the same one twice. Plus, she'll make sure that she's compensated either literally or emotionally for her broken heart. If she's hurt badly enough, she won't forgive or forget. And she shouldn't. After all, if he's been bad enough to kick out, he deserves everything she dishes out.

When her heart is breaking, she will need you to stick close. Invite her over. It's okay to include her whole girl crew too, as being surrounded by her gang makes your Taurus girlfriend feel safe. Break out the pizza and ice cream, because this is one girl who will eat when she's upset.

If you're the one who's crying, this loyal friend will do anything to make you feel better. She can think up exquisitely evil man-tortures that will ultimately make you laugh. Or will hold your hand while you cry, then hand you a tissue and take you out to dinner.

What about the jerk you just broke up with? Well, if he grovels enough you might forgive his slip. Your Taurus chum might not. Ever. If he's been a real bastard, she'll make her feelings clear. Why shouldn't she? She can't stand to see anyone that she cares for hurt or betrayed. If you insist you must give him a second, or third, chance, she'll stand by you. She won't blindly flip her feelings for him or pretend to for you. She isn't made that way.

Guys fall for her friendly demeanor. She's neither too hot nor too aloof, which puts men instantly at ease around her. They start out being friends and end up falling hard. There are two sides to the Taurus romantic nature. One is the ultrafeminine woman who wears silky lingerie and never steps a foot outside without looking model-perfect. The other is the girl-next-door type who might have been a tomboy in school and who's more comfortable wearing jeans as an adult. They display the two faces of Venus—as sex goddess and as Earth mother, but both are physical sensualists.

Neither will try to compete with you. You can trust your guy with this girlfriend. Unless she's blindsided with a soulmate connection, she'll play as fair in love as she does in the other areas of her life.

Bitch Factor

If you always do what interests you,
at least one person is pleased.
CLASSIC MOVIE STAR KATHARINE HEPBURN (MAY 12)

Terrible Taurus traits swing from a near-coma laziness to a reproach-ful composite of those daytime TV judges.

Boring Betty is the classic astrology textbook example of the rut-bound Bull. This girl is so inert that she can barely drag herself to and from work. Her downtime is spent in front of the TV or sleeping, or both. Invite her anywhere and you'll have to plan weeks ahead, then keep reminding her. She's too lazy to write down the date and too brain dead to remember it. Even if she does remember, she might not go, as it's too much trouble to crawl off the couch and into the shower.

Betty is harmless, but she's an excruciating pain in the ass. She can be likable in a strange way, and you might try to change her, at first. Eventually, you'll decide that being friends with her is similar to beating your head against a brick wall. It's a complete waste of time and not worth the pain. Keep her on your Christmas card list if you want to, but don't expect this one to change. She prefers to stay home in her own world. So let her.

The Tightwad takes the Bull's ability to save money and turns it into a peanut-butter-and-jelly nightmare. That's all you'll get in the unlikely event that she happens to invite you over for dinner. The fact that she just spent a zillion dollars on clothes, jewelry, and a side of beef for herself doesn't matter.

She's a user. If you are either well heeled or well connected, expect her to do some major butt kissing to try to win an invitation to hang with your group. She'll try to climb up the ladder on your contacts and push you out of the way as she tramples by. This pretend friend never takes her car because she's always low on gas, never picks up the tab because she forgot her ATM card, and never buys more than a 99-cent birthday card and Dollar Store gift.

Since she's about as subtle as a crutch in her attempts to steal your time and money, it's not hard to figure her out. It won't be hard to dump her off your email list either.

One of the worst women in the zodiac is Judging Jane. She's a raging cow who wants to control the world, you included. Nothing is good enough for Jane. She's permanently pissed and always has at least one enemy that she's trying to destroy.

Jane isn't into stealing your man because no man is good enough for her, especially yours. What she does is run him down while making pretentious comments about how she could do better. She never will, for no one but another loud-mouthed loser will date her.

She's fanatical. Jane has opinions on everything from religion to politics and pushes them on anyone within earshot. She never lets up. This woman would be a dandy organizer for an overzealous group of the obsessively intolerant. One semi-good thing I can say about her is that she hates everyone equally.

Judging Jane is obnoxious and narrow minded. Nothing you can say or do can fix her. The best way to turn her off is to blast back. This bully in a miniskirt has cowed her crowd by operating in wrath mode so long that she's forgotten what it's like to have someone stand up to her. Do it and you'll let the steam out of this windbag. Then step over her and walk on.

Bondability

Sister of the soul: Taurus, Cancer, Pisces
Inner circle: Aries, Virgo, Capricorn
Party pal: Gemini, Libra, Sagittarius
Casual chum: Leo, Scorpio, Aquarius
Famous Taurus friendship: Penelope Cruz and Salma Hayek (a Virgo)

Venus in Taurus

The Venus in Taurus friend has deep feelings and a faithful, loving nature. She's definitely attracted to life's luxuries and can have a tendency to overindulge in anything from food to partying to the sensual pleasures.

A Taurus Venus chum is usually fun to hang around. This placement adds a lighthearted aspect to even the most serious Capricorn, and will help quell the emotional swings of the moodiest Cancer. She'll dispense hugs in large quantities and is sincere and dependable.

Taurus in Venus usually brings some love of nature to every Sun sign personality. She may have a green thumb or keep her home filled with fresh flowers. Her beauty ritual leans toward cleansing products that are non-animal-tested and fragrance free. Her favorite perfumes are usually richly scented and expensive. This girl will sample before she buys and won't spare expense to get the products that appeal to her selective nature.

Her fashion style is based on texture, comfort, and style, and she can shop for days to find the right combination of those three things. Even more than the Taurus Sun, this girlfriend cannot stand itchy fabrics or cheaply made clothes. In her, Venus's discriminating taste is magnified.

Venus here bestows a love of money itself as well as the possessions it can buy. It's also considered a lucky money placement as rewards reaped for this girl's hard work and determination to succeed.

Moon in Taurus

In astrology, the Moon is said to be exalted in Taurus. This means that the combination of Venus-ruled Taurus and the nurturing Moon bestows a calm emotional nature that is gracious and inclined toward friendship. Even the most outgoing Fire Sun will have a serene side to her nature.

This woman is emotionally strong and has loyal, lasting relationships. She has a common-sense outlook and isn't prone to snap judgments or impulsive actions.

Your Taurus Moon pal craves financial security. This aspect will make the most shop-till-you-drop Fire sign more budget conscious, and the flightiest Air sign seek deeper friendships. Taurus is the sign of the collector, and her investment is an emotional one, whether she's acquiring furniture or making lasting relationships.

Taurus's stubbornness also rules, making an Air Sun less rational and a Water Sun more confrontational. Other Earth signs become more set in their ways, while the Fire signs can go ballistic when challenged. This Moon sign can hold a grudge against everyone who's ever pissed her off. However, she will never give up on a relationship until it's been proven to her many times over that either a loved one or a friend has betrayed her.

It's also one of the most controlling aspects. A Taurus Moon girlfriend can be her own worst enemy because of her unwillingness to compromise. However, her generous and good-hearted disposition outweighs her occasional obstinate attitude.

Your Taurus Guy Pal

He's patient, kind hearted, and a little shy. Making friends with a Taurus man might take time, because he's not the type to rush into a relationship or anything else. Once he decides he likes you, he's your friend for life.

A Taurus pal isn't really the work-hard-play-hard type. He's work-hard-then-relax. He'll be happy to meet you for a drink or dinner. He's as generous as Leo, with this difference: he wants to make the offer of help, money, or a kind gesture. If you have to ask him for serious help, do it reluctantly. If he thinks you are using him, he'll drop out of your life.

The Bull isn't subtle. He's not into tossing witty barbs or playing head games. He's honest and appreciates that trait in his friends. If you're in real trouble or have just had your heart broken, he'll be a tower of strength and support. If he's hurting, he won't say much. Don't pry. Do let him know you're there for him.

He might be a handyman type, but if he doesn't like to get his hands dirty, he's sure to know where you can get the best service for the least money.

This quiet guy isn't much for large crowds of anonymous people. Invite him to smaller outings with other close friends. Remember that he's ruled by Venus. Many Taurus men love the fine arts. He'll make a great escort to a concert, theater, or art museum.

Your Taurus guy pal has substance, inner strength, and is one of the most loyal men in the Universe. He'll hang with you in good times or bad, and that's what true friendship is all about.

Chapter Three
Gemini

May 21–June 20
Element: Air
Quality: Mutable
Symbol: The Twins
Ruler: Mercury
Birthstone: Agate
Colors: Yellow, silver-gray, lilac
Flowers: Lily of the valley, lilac, buttercup
Fragrances: Lavender, verbena, sandalwood

Soul Design

Anything that feels that good couldn't possibly be bad.
ACTRESS ANGELINA JOLIE (JUNE 4)

Versatile.

Curious.

Fickle.

Your Gemini girlfriend is curious, funny, and a social butterfly. She has a large group of acquaintances, but very few get inside her inner circle. Gemini loves everyone from a distance. Like her penchant for revolving-door romances, she has a revolving door of new best friends that she crushes on for a few weeks or months, then lets slide down her food chain of relationships. To be her long-term pal, you have to pass a few tests and understand the difference between being close and joined at the hip.

Gemini is ruled by Mercury, the Winged Messenger god who flew all over the Universe with news and gossip. Her home base is the Third House of Communication. Areas included in the Third House are written and verbal self-expression, short trips and everyday travel (to work, school, and errands), and siblings and neighbors. This combination governs your Gemini pal's need to be in constant contact with a variety of people. Her soul is playful. It's shaken off the more serious, possessive outlook of Taurus and rushes headlong into the world with an insatiable desire to experience everything. A Third House soul is like an excitable teenager, and here, every night is Saturday night.

Her soul's purpose is to gather and distribute information. That's the reason your Gemini pal is always on the go. Downtime to a Gemini may mean that she's spending the evening at home, but she's either on the phone or clicking away at email. A Gemini's friends are as varied as her interests in life. She'll know everyone from the paperboy to the mayor, and flow as easily as any Aquarius does between social groups as diverse as the local biker gang or crowd of conservative business people. Want to get the real scoop on what your man does on his night out with the boys? Set your Gemini chum on his trail. Twins were born to spy, and most have an uncanny sixth sense about where to go to discover the dirt.

friends on a Rotten Day

This doesn't mean that she's a gossipy airhead. Your Gemini pal is a quick learner who will know how to program her TiVo and fix a leaky faucet. She likes the challenge of learning something new. She also will put her analytical skills to work to help you solve either a career or personal problem.

She's a natural teacher. Her opposite sign, Sagittarius, may be the philosopher of the zodiac, but your Twin chum is concerned with how to make everyday life easier. Whether it's a state-of-the-art cell phone, better Internet service, or the latest diet, she wants to know the best way to save time and effort on the mundane. She'll share what she's learned with you. As this girlfriend isn't the most naturally detail-oriented person on the planet, I wouldn't advise that you rush out to buy, sign up, or switch to anything new until you've read the fine print. Gemini is great at changing her mind. She might come back a few days later to announce she's dumped the first hot idea in favor of a new, better one. It will save you a headache and some hard-earned cash if you do your own research. Stay on her speed-dial list by keeping up with the latest news, time-saving tips, or tools. If you can manage to discover something new to share with her first, you'll earn buddy bonus points.

As a *Masculine Mutable Air* sign, she is assertive and not afraid to tell you if something bothers her. She is as curious as Aquarius and as analytical as Libra. Her Mutable side sets her apart in that she is flexible. She can appreciate differing points of view, and she usually doesn't mind those last-minute plan changes. She's also a champ at arguing her point and talking people into doing what she wants.

Her symbol of Twin souls standing side by side not only represents her dual nature, but doubles her Air sign penchant for chatter. She's as talkative as her opposite, Sagittarius, but where the Archer will go into great detail to collect and share her information, Gemini skims the surface. Ever been bombarded with Gemini questions? If she's truly excited, she will fire off a question, try to guess your answer, then shoot another at you before you've had time to think. This isn't snoopiness for gossip's sake, as she's often astrologically painted, but her need to get all the details in the shortest possible time.

She's the multi-tasking champion of the zodiac. Whether she's juggling parties, lovers, or more than one career, a Gemini chum thrives on keeping busy. When she's really interested, she can learn twice as much in half the time as most of the rest of us.

Astronaut Sally Ride's first love was tennis. She won a tennis scholarship in high school, then later dropped out of college to pursue a career as a professional tennis player. After a few months, Ride decided the pro circuit wasn't for her, so she enrolled at Stanford University. By the time she was twenty-seven, she'd earned a BA, BS, and Master's degree in astrophysics. She was a PhD candidate when she applied to NASA's space program. In 1983, Dr. Ride became the first American woman in space. She retired from NASA at age thirty-seven. Some of her achievements since then include serving as the director of the California Space Institute, professor of physics at the University of California at San Diego, executive VP and board member of *space.com,* and founder of the EarthKAM NASA project that allows middle school classes to photograph the Earth from outer space. With typical Gemini enthusiasm, she's on a mission to educate and support all girls who are interested in science, math, and the technical fields.

The leap from professional tennis player to astronaut might seem impossible, even laughable for some other signs. It's a perfect example of what a Gemini in high gear can accomplish.

Most Twins are natural mimics and love word play. As does Pisces, she'll make up code names for various people, including you, and is a whiz at pun making. Her gift for imitation is guaranteed to make you laugh. On another level of imitation as admiration, she could start to wear her hair like yours, buy her clothes at your favorite store, or even pick up your conversational style. This doesn't mean that she wants to be you. It's an unconscious trait. When she feels close to someone, she often assumes a few of that person's qualities.

After the initial my-new-best-friend burst of closeness, she'll want to spend more time with her other friends. This doesn't mean she likes you less. Your Gemini pal may consider you to be a best buddy, but she's absolutely not the type to relish a one-on-one friendship for long. She's more apt to have a best friend for each sector of her life. Most likely, you'll be her best clubbing friend, or her best gym buddy, or her confidant when she's upset. She needs the initial closeness to discover which sector you fit into. Of all the signs, Gemini is the least likely to have one forever friend that she hangs with to the exclusion of her other pals. Pinned down to one person in any capacity is not a natural state for a Gemini soul.

She can be too trusting. A Gemini heart is as big as a Leo's. The difference is that she accepts everyone she likes at face value. She'll fall into your friendship as hard and fast as she falls in love. That's why she sometimes gets involved with characters who take advantage of her liberal nature. She can get hurt, but unlike a Water sign that can wallow in its misery, she'll bounce back fast and move on to her next adventure. Her philosophy is one of not wasting time on things she can't change.

Your Gemini best friend is versatile and creative. She can be exasperating when she's arguing you into the ground trying to make a point, and she may occasionally flake out on you. She has a special talent for knowing how to cheer you up when you're blue, and she'll never lose her teenage-like enthusiasm for life. Being her friend can be like riding a whirlwind. You might not know where you'll end up, but you're guaranteed not to ever be bored.

Groove Meter

I was always the little entertainer.
ACTRESS NATALIE PORTMAN (JUNE 9)

Anything that doesn't involve sitting still is fun to a Gemini woman. She dislikes doing things alone, so you can even call her to go grocery shopping, especially if it's a megafoods store with at least one section of exotic or unusual items. Like every girl, she'll love to hit the mall with you—if you know where you're going. She's not into spending all day window shopping or wandering through every store at the outlet center. She wants to get in, buy what she's after, and get out so that she has time to do some other fun thing such as having lunch at the newest restaurant in town.

Want to take a class at the local adult school? Whether it's creative writing, watercolor painting, or fortune telling, call her. Your Gemini pal is always eager to learn something new. She'll dive in and become an instant, if temporary, expert on whatever the subject is, then have great fun entertaining your mutual friends with what she's learned. Want a gym buddy? She'll go with you, but don't expect her to like the routine of treadmill, weight machines, and shower. Instead try something unusual, and the newer the better. She likes to keep up on the latest trends.

Every Gemini has a childlike quality about her. Don't confuse this with the sometimes childish behavior of other signs, such as Aries, which can be embarrassing. Gemini's tendency to have a spirit of fun and mischief her entire life gives her the aura of eternal youth. Although it's a fact that many Geminis don't have families, or have small ones, your Gemini friend will probably adore kids, and they adore her. Even at seventy, she has the unique ability to remember what it's like to be one. The generation gap doesn't seem to exist for this woman.

She's another friend who's great to take on a road trip. A vacation where you stay one or two days each in a variety of locations will suit her perfectly. If you're into soaking up the sun while vegging on the beach, take your Taurus, Leo, or Pisces buddies. A Gemini girl wants to see, taste, touch, and experience everything on vacation, as she does everywhere else. She'll probably bring a camera to record the fun. Her mischievous side won't be able to resist snapping a few candid shots if she can, so beware of open shower doors or dancing on a table if you get wasted.

If the party's for her, invite as many of her other friends as you can find. She's one sign that may or may not like true surprises, so you'll have to get to know her preferences. That's easy. Ask her. Well in advance of when you might expect to plan a celebration for her. Whether it's casual or formal, consider a buffet versus sit-down dinner, so that she can circulate among her chums.

She's one of the easiest signs to buy for. She'll like a book, CD, DVD, or the latest techno, kitchen, or time-saving gadget. Gift cards are great because she gets to choose. Incense or aromatherapy scents will soothe her sometimes jangled nerves. She'll adore opening lots of little inexpensive gifts.

If she's getting married, and depending upon how deep her experimental side is, she'll like anything from an herb garden to a gift card to the adult toy shop. She'll appreciate a cookbook that's full of time-saving recipes that she can whip up on a moment's notice.

She's full of life and mischief. Your Gemini BFF is an ageless wonder who's on a never-ending quest for discovery. Take her anywhere, and you'll both have a ball.

Speed Bumps

You and me and everyone else is guilty of the crime . . .
which is morbid curiosity about someone else's life.
ACTRESS ELIZABETH HURLEY (JUNE 10)

Gemini Air is restless. Your Gemini girlfriend usually has so many projects going at once that she often juggles her calendar. She may change lunch dates several times, show up an hour late to dinner, or cancel a night out because she's overbooked and decides that another party will be more fun. The upside is that she'll invite you to the bash. This might not be too consoling, especially if you hate last-minute plan changes. On the other hand, this is a perfect example of her unpredictable nature, and, as often as not, the switch will be as much fun as whatever you had planned.

The more flexible you can be with a Gemini pal, the less likely you are to lose your cool. She hates to make anyone feel bad. She also has an *oh, well* attitude about pissing you or anyone off.

She's born with a near-insatiable curiosity. To her, the shortest distance to knowledge is a direct question. Remember this fact when you get the feeling that she's prying or getting too personal too fast. Remember, too, that this girlfriend appreciates and understands a direct answer. No. You aren't ready to discuss whatever it is she's asked about. The caveat is that she'll keep trying, like the proverbial kid who continually asks, "Why?" This can get really annoying, especially when a month, or a year, later she brings up the subject again. She's not above trying to trick you, such as blindsiding you with a question when it's the last thing on your mind. If she can get the details by catching you off guard, she'll do it. So, if the issue is a burning one that you absolutely do not want to share, you'll need to keep a few brain cells on alert for these out-of-the-blue quizzes.

Because she is one of the easiest signs to talk to, your initial reaction is to trust her and spill your guts. Even if you're a private Scorpio or reserved Capricorn, her disarming way of opening up about herself will have you sharing a secret or two. She can bare the skeletons in her family closet and tell you how her last lover was hung nearly in the same breath. One caution is that, as free as she is with her own history, she can also be free with yours should the subject come up in another conversation. If you want to keep your stories confidential, you'll need to say that upfront. Even then, be careful, for she can blurt out a secret before she stops to think. You have to decide how much you want her to know. It's her soul's perspective to exchange information, and most Gemini pals have few secrets. Chances are, yours might come out sooner or later, at least to one of your other close friends.

To her, sharing intimate details bonds your friendship. What she does is hint, broadly and long, to another person. *I know something you don't.* And the more the other person plays along, the broader the hints become. A Gemini pal's weakness is not being able to keep her mouth shut, either with a juicy story or something that she thinks might have value for another person. Typically, she's not malicious. As she gets older, she's usually better at understanding and respecting other people's privacy.

She is paranoid. This is her most exasperating trait because, when she's in this mode, she can resort to lying, manipulating, and being so evasive that she won't tell you what she had for lunch. Don't buy into her angst. If you ask a question and, instead of getting an answer, you get a one-word reply, drop the subject. Otherwise, she'll make you play Twenty Questions while she's trying to decide whether you're up to something.

If she's jealous because you and a mutual friend went to lunch without her, she could act like a homicide detective trying to crack a case. You might think she's cracking up. Again, this has nothing to do with you. She's operating from her lesser Twin side—the one that either is panicked that you're not truly a friend, but only using her, or is obsessed with "catching" you in a betrayal. If you like her and want to remain friends, you have to be the rational one. She won't be, and arguing with her will cause a rift. Later, she'll most likely apologize with an offhand remark or, more likely, by taking you to lunch or bringing you a small gift. Accept it and forget her lapse. She will. It's the worst bump she'll cause in your friendship road, and if you'll admit it, you've tossed a couple of your own rocks in the path too.

Romance Rating

What do I wear in bed?
Why Chanel No 5, of course.
CLASSIC MOVIE STAR MARILYN MONROE (JUNE 1)

Your Gemini girlfriend frequently gets her heart broken because she falls in and out of love at the speed of light. She's friendly, flirty, and can be one of the worst judges of man-character in the Universe. She has the unique perspective of expecting her boyfriends to be mind readers. She'll complain that her last three lovers totally misunderstood her, but she won't have taken the time to talk to them about her needs and expectations. Seem contradictory for a girl who can out-talk a Sagittarius? It is. While she is great at analyzing the issues, one of her weaknesses is a lack of introspection.

Being an Air sign, she's not likely to hold anything back when venting about what went wrong. Even if she's happy with her new man, she'll keep returning to the problems with the old one. Listening is the best thing you can do. You'll need patience, as she can get as obsessive as any Water sign over who did what to whom and endlessly rehash the situation.

She won't expect you to rescue her. Usually because she'll have another guy lined up to do that before her tears are dried. A Gemini girl usually goes for the man-sampler-plate instead of sticking out the seven-course dinner of a long-term relationship. Of course, not every Gemini woman has revolving-door relationships, especially as they get older and wiser. I'll bet you, though, that every one of your Gemini pals has been in love with more guys than most of your other girlfriends, including you.

If you need her, all you have to do is call. Your Gemini pal will fix you a bed on the couch or come over and spend the night at your place. She'll do anything to cheer you up. She'll let you vent and agree with every word you say. She'll use her talent for mimicry to try to make you laugh by imitating the man who broke your heart. As an Air sign, she operates from an intellectual versus emotional viewpoint. Instead of putting her arms around you like a Water sign would, or offering the practical advice of an Earth sign, your Gemini friend's irreverent, even inappropriate remarks are meant to help. If you're singing the blues, her actions might seem thoughtless. Don't misunderstand. She's totally sympathetic. She simply doesn't understand wallowing in emotional turmoil. It goes against her nature. She can get very uncomfortable if you're sobbing your heart out on her couch, and making light of a bad situation works for her. One caveat: she's not above doing this in front of him as your private "joke" if you make up. She thinks it's hilarious. You be on guard.

My Gemini best friend and I made a pact long ago concerning guys. *If you love him, I love him. If you hate him, I hate him.* It's a great idea. It also says everything about friendship with a Gemini. Other girlfriends might feel the need to remind you of what a bastard your ex is and warn you not to give him a second chance. Your Gemini pal will be as ready to forgive him as you are if you decide to take him back. She does it for your sake.

Remember this when she decides to give her ex another try. Or tells you that she hates her current lover with a passion over coffee at 10 A.M., then calls you that evening declaring her undying adoration for the guy. If you try to remind her that he was an unforgivable jerk a few hours ago, she'll bombard you with a hundred justifications for his action. Plus a hundred reasons why he's really the Best Man Alive. Every Gemini's boyfriend is a BMA. She has to feel he's powerful, smart, funny, and better than any other man, including yours. Once she dumps him, he'll become a WBB, World's Biggest Bastard.

Just as she likes a variety of girlfriends, your Gemini pal does not stick to one type of guy. The Daddy, the Bad Boy, the Intellectual, the Loser—each one of these dudes can make her tumble into a hot, and frequently, disastrous affair. It's also the reason for the Gemini divorce rate, which is probably higher than the national average. Along with Scorpio, Capricorn, and Pisces, she frequently gets caught up in what she wants the relationship to be instead of reality. Marilyn Monroe is perhaps the most famously fractured Gemini in recent history. Her man woes are legendary. Multiple broken marriages, scandalous liaisons with powerful men on both sides of the law, and an eternally lost-little-girl outlook made her a sad figure despite her tremendous movie star success.

Your Gemini pal will probably not have as messy a love life, but she can be on a daddy search for the one man who'll make her feel protected and pampered no matter how badly she behaves. Gemini women who date father figures are operating on dual control: wanting to have her man and keep one foot in the dating pool, or wanting a stable home that she can escape to when her social life gets too messy. She can run home, slam the door, and Big Daddy will see to it that she's not disturbed.

She won't subject herself to much emotional expression and won't be able to tolerate it from any of her men. She'll try, although no Air sign is comfortable in dealing with blatant feelings. This doesn't mean that she's not romantic. Her ideal is that of a lighthearted romantic comedy, full of witty conversation, flirty eye contact, and glamour. Her love style is a catch-me-if-you-can game that, in her eyes, should last forever.

Unfortunately, most of the men she picks are the opposite. She seems to be drawn to drama kings, suffering artists, or men with various types of addictions. She's one of the zodiac's fixers. She'll try anything in her arsenal of ideas and intellect to change or save the guy, but what she ends up doing is fleeing from the excess emotion.

If she does get hooked by a guy who expects her to carry his emotional needs or turn her into an everywoman wife and mother, she'll become the most miserable creature around. She will never learn to enjoy the manipulating head games that many people play, even though she will try hard to meet him halfway, for a while. Eventually, she'll leave. Usually, she'll have his replacement waiting in the wings. You'll hold your breath, hoping he's better than the one she's just kicked out.

It may take her half a lifetime but, sooner or later, most Gemini women find the right combination of friendship and deep love. That's because no matter how much she blasts the idea of true love, she rarely gives up until she finds it.

Bitch Factor

I think if you have the opportunity to bully your opponent,
you have to take that chance.
TENNIS STAR VENUS WILLIAMS (JUNE 17)

Unevolved Geminis have a variety of bad behaviors, from bimbo, to liar, to manipulator.

The Parrot is the least harmful and most annoying Gemini. More bimbo than bitch, she's the reason the word *airhead* was coined. She overflows with opinions. Listen carefully and you'll quickly discover that like her namesake, she's mimicking everything you say. Bashing a mutual acquaintance? The Parrot will jump in with both feet to join the gossip. Change your position and she'll instantly change hers, spouting why she thinks that the person is so wonderful. More time-sucking bore than dangerous adversary, her Gemini energy field is so scattered that she can't formulate her own thought. Tell her you're in a meeting every day at 9 A.M. and she'll call precisely at that time. This one pretends to be interested in everything from your friendship to saving the world. Her real motive is to try to force herself into your inner circle by sheer will and a never-ending siege on your good nature.

This dumb bunny cozies up to you because you're smart, popular, have a hot car or career. She only wants to be friends because she envies you or wants something you have. Like a used car salesman, she'll promise you the Moon, but try to collect and she'll have a hundred lame excuses why she can't really help you move or follow through on a pre-agreed plan. She's so high maintenance and lazy that she'd rather waste both your time and hers asking you to figure out how to work her new cell phone instead of reading the instructions. She can ask the same question a hundred times and never seems to get the answer. Unless you're on drugs, you shouldn't have trouble spotting or avoiding this one. Send her calls to voicemail and don't answer her e-mails. Sooner or later, she'll get the hint and go plague someone else.

Next on the Gemini bad-girl list is the Brat. No matter what her age, her emotional level is that of the perennial push-for-limits teenager. Operating in permanent angst mode, the Brat rails at everything from social injustice to the unlucky waiter who happened to deliver her lunch. Her idea of friendship is keeping her inner circle close by intimidation. Lies are as natural to her as breathing is to the rest of us. She'll worm her way into a power position by using the Gemini fine art of conversation to make her girlfriends think she's interested in them. What she really wants is the license to act as irresponsibly as she pleases while expecting everyone to remain doggishly devoted to her. Dogs are about the only friends who last with this bad girl. Everyone else soon tires of the hurtful put-downs and mean-spirited comments that she tries to pass off as jokes, her embarrassing public behavior, and the constant two-faced gossip behind their backs.

Push the Brat to the nth degree and you end up with Narcissistic Nancy. She could be the worst bitch in the entire zodiac. She's dangerous, because she's often so slick that before you realize what's happening, you've been sucked into one of her endless mind games. Say,

"Hi," and she'll question your motives. Ask her a question and she'll deride you for being stupid.

At work, she's the one who'll collect a pile of the company's dirty laundry and use it to climb up the corporate ladder. Personally, she'll not only flirt with your man right under your nose like some other bad girls, but she's ballsy enough to give him her cell number while you're standing there. Then tell him to call her on the pretext of an innocent conversation while silently daring you to say anything. Any man is fair game, relatives included, if she happens to like her brother-in-law. She tries to put people in lose-lose positions. It makes her feel powerful. Don't try to fight her; she feeds on a feud.

Nancy is malicious, spiteful, and one smooth operator. She's the original silver-tongued devil and she causes serious damage wherever she lands. Be wary if she rushes to become your new best friend. Pretend you're a Scorpio when she's picking your brain for secrets. Trust your gut with this one. If it feels like you've been mind-screwed, you have. Run, don't walk, to the nearest exit.

Bondability

Sister of the soul: Gemini, Aquarius
Inner circle: Leo, Taurus, Libra
Party pal: Aries, Scorpio, Sagittarius, Pisces
Casual chum: Cancer, Virgo, Capricorn
Famous Gemini friendship: Courtney Cox-Arquette and Jennifer Aniston (an Aquarius)

II

Venus in Gemini

In Gemini, Venus loves variety. This girlfriend appreciates the differences of her friends and has a sociable and flirty edge to her personality no matter what her Sun sign. She's open, witty, and attracts people from all walks of life. Venus here adds a chatty trait to even the quietest Scorpio. This aspect can also add a bit of superficiality to the Sun sign character, which might make an Air sign even more aloof or a Water sign less emotional.

This placement bestows a quick mind and talent for turning the ordinary into something special. It also can make her a little too quick to grab for the brass ring when, with a little more forethought and patience, she could have the pot of gold at the end of the rainbow.

Gemini Venus pals can be excitable and eager to try new things. This girl might spend a lot of time and money on the Home Shopping channel getting hooked on the latest gadgets or newest beauty fad. This isn't the trendsetter style of Aries Venus. In Gemini, Venus is like a kid who wants to sample all the candy in the store.

Her fashion sense is eclectic, and even the most classically chic Capricorn is likely to have a few pieces of the latest fashion craze hanging in her closet.

A Gemini Venus girlfriend usually likes to travel and might even make her living from the vacation industry. She will also have some natural inclination to the Mercury-ruled talent for communication.

Moon in Gemini

Gemini Moons are ingenious, intellectual, versatile, and responsive. They are also restless, nervous, and emotionally inconsistent.

This Moon loves to be entertained and is so easily bored that you might have to run to keep up with even the most laid-back Virgo or otherwise stay-at-home Scorpio. A Gemini Moon is a challenge to any Sun sign, as it exacerbates the duality of Gemini. This girl can shock you by being the model of manners one day and deciding to hit a nudie beach the next. Her emotional swings aren't from good to bad, but from tame to rowdy.

A Gemini Moon adds a clever ability to persuade others to her way of thinking, but with a much more subtle flair than the Gemini Sun. Girlfriends with this placement can lay awake nights plotting their next moves because they love to be in control. However, this isn't meant maliciously. The vast majority of these girlfriends use this talent to try to help solve problems for their friends and family. However, most end up in a soap opera of emotional tangles.

This Moon adds a sympathetic, receptive nature to the Sun sign personality. It lessens the quarrelsome aspects of quick-tempered Aries and critical Virgo. Any girlfriend with a Gemini Moon will have an irresistibly mischievous aspect to her personality that makes her part angel, part devil, and always on the go.

Your Gemini Guy Pal

A fun-loving Gemini guy has a wicked wit and devilishly sarcastic view of the world. Even though you're just pals, he can't resist flirting with you. He isn't above making naughty comments about how hot you look or what you might be doing with your latest boyfriend.

He's a natural politician who can see both sides of any situation. He loves a good debate, so don't be afraid to argue with him over anything. Take either side you want, because this guy usually can argue both points of view with equal skill.

Your Gemini buddy has a deep understanding and appreciation for human nature. He values friendship and will be there for you in spirit, if not in body. He's a great play pal, but you can't really count on him to always show up when he says that he will. So save the must-be-there dates for your Earth buddies.

Take him to your company picnic or to the office Christmas party. He'll impress your boss and coworkers with his easy conversation style and the interest he shows in their careers. It's real. Even if he's not a deep thinker, he's superficially interested in everything and genuinely likes talking to people.

While he's not nearly as private as Scorpio or Capricorn, he is evasive. You can never be sure when he'll answer a question. He might start a verbal sparring match. He might lie. He might pretend he's gone deaf and ignore it all together. It depends on his whim of the moment. Don't sweat it. It's one of his quirks, and he's full of them.

One day he's the class clown, the next an offbeat poet, the day after that a Boy Scout helping old ladies and rescuing stray dogs. He's full of personalities, and even he doesn't know who's about to pop out next. That's his charm, and your luck.

Chapter Four
Cancer

June 21–July 22
Element: Water
Quality: Cardinal
Symbol: The Crab
Ruler: The Moon
Birthstone: Pearl
Colors: Gray-greens, silver
Flowers: Larkspur, lotus, water lily
Fragrances: Tea rose, night-blooming jasmine, gardenia

Soul Design

*It's not the load that breaks you down,
it's the way you carry it.*
SINGER LENA HORNE (JUNE 30)

Caring.

Loyal.

Touchy.

Cancer girlfriends often get a bad rap because many astrology books dwell on the moodiness of this sign. As one of the Water signs, she feels emotions deeply, as do sisters Pisces and Scorpio. However, she's not the whiny reclusive manipulator she's been called. Your Cancer girlfriend is resilient, sympathetic, and has a tremendous inner strength. True, her surface temperament can be as changeable as the phases of her ruler, the Moon. Inside, this woman is one tough cookie who rarely crumbles.

She's *Feminine Cardinal Water*. As a Cardinal sign she likes to lead and initiate the action, like the other Cardinal signs of Aries, Libra, and Capricorn. As a Feminine sign, she's more apt to use subtle tactics to get what she wants. Her Water nature adds emotion to the mix, and her symbol the Crab means that she rarely takes the direct path anywhere. A better description of her character might be to say that she's both coy and crafty.

Your Cancer girlfriend's soul lives in the Fourth House of Home, Past, Present, and Future. Having moved here from the energy-charged pad of gadabout Gemini, she's had it with nonstop talking and shallow relationships. The soul quiets down in this cozy crib and forms more intimate bonds in relationships. In the Fourth House it's always family night, and the Cancer soul is the nurturing parent. A Fourth House home doesn't necessarily mean bricks and mortar. Cancers are as prone to physically moving as any other sign, and contrary to popular belief, not all are domestic. Think of a real crab. Some carry their homes on their backs, some move from rock to rock on the beach, and some live deep in the ocean, hidden from view.

A Cancer woman doesn't necessarily need biological family ties. What she does need is an emotional link, whether to a traditional family, a childhood memory, or her current group of friends. Without emotional connections she's largely lost and often depressed.

Cancer chums thrive on being needed. That's why she hovers. She's not trying to control your life for any dark or unscrupulous reason. She'll bring you chicken soup when you're ill and feed your animals while you're on vacation. She'll also worry if you don't check in with her on a regular basis. One way to keep high on her best pal list is to simply keep in touch, and not only with chatty news or the neighborhood gossip. Cancer chums aren't too interested in the superficial or into the grapevine gab as much as most of the rest of us. She's concerned with your personal life and hers. She likes to know what's going on with you and to help you fix anything that isn't going well. Remember that Abigail Van Buren (Dear Abby) and her twin, Ann Landers, were born under the sign of the Crab.

When I left home and moved into my first apartment, I had a Cancer friend who lived about a hundred miles away. She was a pal of my oldest brother, was divorced with two small children, and worked two jobs to survive. She also appointed herself as my big sister. She would call me a couple of times a week, and her first words were always, "How are you doing? Do you need anything?" She made curtains for my small apartment and drove up to help me hang them. No matter how busy she was, she always had time to help, listen, and to do thoughtful things. She made me and everyone around her feel loved and appreciated.

Your Cancer girlfriend won't fail to ask if your child is over her cold or how your job search is going. She'll want to know how you feel and whether you've had your checkup. Keep her close by being interested in her personal life. She's a natural caregiver, but sometimes we can forget that she needs to be nurtured too.

She rarely lets go of anything. Most of us keep some memorabilia of our childhoods. Cancer, along with sister Taurus, can be one of the zodiac's hoarders. From something as mundane as a ball of rubber bands from the morning paper to a list of her ex-lovers' phone numbers, she'll usually hang onto a mishmash of junk that has meaning only to her. This isn't the security-building of the Bull. The box of old letters or that deposit receipt from her first apartment are the emotional ties to a Cancer chum's past. These are the links that form the continuity of the sense of home that her soul needs.

Yes, she has mood swings. Ruled by the Moon, her moods are extremely changeable. Think of the way the Moon pulls at the tides and how it goes from hidden to full in its monthly cycle. Her emotions are in a constant cyclic motion as well, and she'll be the first to tell you that she can be as confused by them as you. I had a Cancer chum in high school who could walk into the last five seconds of a tearjerker movie and start crying. She didn't know the plot. She hadn't a clue as to what was going on, but her tears would flow. Most of us will do that now and then. But, if you kept score, I'll bet you'd discover that a Cancer pal would win the Most Sentimental Girl award, hands down.

This girlfriend is neither a weepy-eyed sob sister nor at the mercy of her hormones, as she's sometimes portrayed. She is certainly sensitive, but she tries hard to keep on an even keel. Unless you belong to her inner circle, you might never suspect that she's feeling anything but happy and upbeat.

As Libra will, a Cancer friend might put you through a series of little tests to see if you will fit into her closest-chums club. She might ask you to feed her cat over the weekend. Or ask you for a ride to your girls'-night-out dinner. Or share one of her small dilemmas to check your rating on her empathy scale. She doesn't do this because she feels superior or to see if you measure up to some sort of friendship standard. She's operating from her timid Crab side. She feels you out. Is it safe to confide in you, trust you, depend on you? She moves sideways in building relationships the same way a real crab moves across the beach. She may zigzag, but she's always in forward motion.

Your Cancer friend may have the looniest sense of humor under the Sun. Think of comic legend Phyllis Diller and her endless putdowns of her husband, "Fang." Or Gilda Radner from the classic

Saturday Night Live comedy show. As does sister Capricorn, your Cancer girlfriend can shock you with a hilarious, off-the-wall remark that seems out of character. It isn't. She's so attuned to life that she can see all of the flaws and absurdities of personal relationships.

When she is down, a change of scenery can help to restore her smile. Just as Earth and Fire signs like the outdoors and Air signs like to circulate with people, Water signs are revived by being near water. Take her on a day trip to the nearest beach, or if you're landlocked, to a water park or mountain stream. The rhythmic patterns of the waves or the consistency of the stream's movement over the rocks soothes her. When you're down, she'll invite you to her place for tea and home-baked cookies. She'll cry, laugh, and sympathize with you.

All Water signs need periods of solitude. Pisces retreats. Scorpio can brood. When your Cancer girlfriend seems withdrawn, it's usually because she's going through a period of change. It could be anything from a relationship breakup to making a career change to deciding to move. This is when her reclusive side appears. She might not answer the phone, or she will go incommunicado for a couple of days. Three things occur when this happens. While the other Water sisters are aware of their need to withdraw, your Cancer girlfriend is operating on instinct, so it isn't necessarily a conscious decision. As a Cardinal sign, she'll prefer to work out the solution on her own. And her Fourth House soul-as-big-mama feels that she should be able to handle it alone.

There's not much you can do when she's in full retreat except respect her need for privacy and let her know you are there for her. Leave a voicemail or email her, whether or not she answers. When she does stick her head out again, you'll be the first person she'll want to see.

Your Cancer pal is a total sentimentalist. Everything affects her in some way. She might give her last dollar to a homeless person. She'll make your personal business hers and expect you to take her advice.

She's friend, sister, mother all rolled together. She can't separate one from the other, and you can't change her. Her need to nurture is soul deep. Even if it is sometimes annoying, look on the bright side. At least she truly cares about you. In today's world, having a friend who is that loyal and concerned is priceless.

Groove Meter

My ideal relaxation is working on upholstery.
I spend hours in junk shops buying furniture.
ACTRESS PAMELA ANDERSON (JULY 1)

Your Cancer BFF isn't the most social creature on the zodiac family tree, and most likely won't be committed to the party hardy lifestyle. If you're a where's-the-action Fire sign, or an Airy social butterfly, don't take it personally when she passes on a paint-the-town-red night out. This chum loves to spend time at home. It really is where her heart is, whether she's still living with her parents, is married, or has her own place.

She's not a prude by any means. Neither is she aloof or lazy. She has a definite boogie switch, but she doesn't flip it on as often as some of your other girlfriends. When she does, she can get down all night long. But it's unlikely that you will see her constantly on the dance floor or swirling through an endless stream of parties, even during the holidays.

If she's your best friend, she'll prefer one-on-one outings. Dinner, shopping, day trips, all the usual stuff, but it's more fun for her when it's close and personal. That way she has your entire attention. Have two tickets to a play? Call her. Want to go to the garden shop? She'll look at every plant with you and probably buy something for her own yard or windowsill.

Your Cancer chum usually likes to entertain at home, which is no surprise if you've ever known one. If she's into cooking, this pal can whip up a fabulous dinner for her friends, even on a thin budget. She'll pay attention to every detail, from the place settings to the best wine that she can afford. Want to organize a day at the beach or in the park for your crew? Put your Cancer girlfriend in charge of the food. Even if it's grilled hamburgers, she'll add special touches like a variety of gourmet cheeses, or an exotic cold salad that she found at a local deli.

Because of her soul's attachment to the past, she's another woman that you can take antique shopping. Most Cancer friends will trek with you to visit an historical site, whether it's local or a vacation to the ruins of an ancient civilization.

One of her more peculiar traits is that occasionally, she'll flake on a night out. She might call you at the last minute or simply not show up. Unlike Gemini's tendency to overbook, a Cancer girl has probably decided that she'd rather stay home. Maybe her favorite old movie is on TV or she's decided she wants to finish her latest romance novel or she's gotten comfortable on the sofa with her cat.

Sometimes she gets a little too homebound. It's okay to insist that she get out of the house. Tell her that you miss her and entice her with the latest romantic comedy or salad bar dinner followed by dessert at her favorite ice cream shop.

Planning her birthday? Have the party at either your place or another one of her close friend's. She'll be much more relaxed and comfortable when it's only her and her best pals.

Cancer girlfriends will appreciate almost any gift, because you took time to think of her. Since she loves making memories, a camera is a good choice. If you get her one, have her open it first, then ask another friend to snap pics of the party. A disposable one will work if you're on a budget. Picture frames or a personalized photo album are good choices, since she's likely to have a box filled with snapshots stashed in her closet. An album already filled with photos of you and her other pals will make her laugh and cry at the same time.

A book on decorating, cooking, or gardening will appeal to her. If it's a novel, try an historical romance. For fun, give her a piggy bank for her change. Crabs are always saving for a special purchase or the proverbial rainy day. Plants are great, or a gift certificate to the local nursery if she has a garden.

If it's her bridal shower, again, have it at someone's home. She'll love practical gifts such as his-and-hers matching bath towels or kitchen gadgets. If it's a lingerie shower, appeal to her naughty side—and she definitely has one, no matter what her age—with a nearly sheer nightgown or a lacy teddy.

She's always up for any outing that includes water-based fun such as sailing, water skiing, or a pool party. If you go to the beach, she probably will prefer to walk the shoreline collecting seashells rather than baking on a blanket in the sun.

She'll bring back a souvenir from every place you go to. She'll keep them all until you're both old, and when you go to her house for dinner she'll bring them out so that you can relive each fun moment.

Speed Bumps

Being good is just a matter of temperament in the end.
IRISH AUTHOR IRIS MURDOCH (JULY 15)

All Water signs operate from a feelings-first perspective. Your Cancer pal can act paranoid over things that probably won't ever happen. Her greatest angst comes from either being ignored or feeling that the situation is beyond her control.

The husband of a Cancer coworker of mine often traveled on charitable missions to Third World countries. Although he was connected with a large organization and never went into dangerous areas, my Cancer friend always panicked about what *might* happen. Until she got his phone call assuring her that he was safe at his destination, she drove herself and the rest of us batty with her unfounded fear. Yes, you know that she really has no control over anything except her own emotional reactions. She doesn't often figure that out. That's why it's kinder for you to at least thank her and say that you'll consider her advice, or to text her that you're alive and well on vacation. Do it, even if you're a Fire sign and think she's gone completely crazy.

On the flip side, it's hard to give this girlfriend advice because, as a Cardinal sign, she has a built-in resistance to having anyone suggest that she needs it. Compound this by thinking of your real mom. How often does she take advice from her kids?

Then how can you help her? Listen. Schedule a wine-and-vent date, then let her roll through whatever emotional turmoil she's feeling. She'll laugh, cry, and fume. Whether or not you offer advice isn't important. That you are there to comfort her and hear her story is crucial.

She's a natural meddler. While your Leo friend meddles because it makes her feel powerful, Cancer believes she's doing it for your own good. Like a good mother who has your best interests at heart, a Cancer pal's motto could be *I know best*. Of course, she doesn't know any more than the rest of us, as her messy life sometimes proves. That won't stop her from giving you advice or occasionally and irritatingly treating you as if you really were a child. When she's in smother-mother mode, the wisest thing you can do is to gently but firmly make a boundary. Always thank her first. Give her a hug. Tell her how much you appreciate her. Then remind her that, in this case, you've made the decision. Be warned. This probably won't stop her from trying to convince you to see things her way. She's not a girl who gives up easily. Keep your mental armor on so that you can resist that gentle, but oh-so-firm pressure.

A Cancer friend of mine once tried to convince me that we should go into business together. Although her idea was fun—creating slogan T-shirts—neither of us had the time or resources to handle this project. Plus, I wasn't really interested. I tried each one of the reasons, but being the tenacious little Crab she is, she kept trying, and trying, and trying to convince me we would make tons of money. Finally, I had to just tell her, "No"—nicely, of course, because she is a great pal. With that declaration, she appeared to let up. What she was really doing was changing tactics and zigzagging into manipulation mode.

Emotional blackmail is your Cancer's pal's ace in the hole. When all else fails, she won't hesitate to try to make you feel guilty if she's determined to get her own way. It's martyr mode, and although all Water signs are good at it, and Taurus and Libra occasionally slip into it, your Cancer pal is a world-class champion.

Suppose you have a girls' night out planned and a conflict arises in her calendar. Instead of telling you she's sorry and to have fun without her as a Fire sign would, or that she'll try to come late if she can as an Air sign would, a Cancer girl will try to get your group to rearrange everyone else's schedule to accommodate her. She'll do this by playing the martyr. If only there was a way to make it work. You know how much she loves it when the group gets together. Maybe something can be done.

Each of these statements are accompanied by a sad look and pregnant pause designed to let you step in and offer to cancel the evening and reschedule when she is available. She will never directly ask; that's too crass. She won't hesitate to try to make you feel guilty about having fun without her.

My friend used martyr mode as her last resort regarding the T-shirt business. She needed the money and thought this would be a fun way to make extra cash. The guilty implication for me was that if I didn't jump into this venture with her, she might starve.

I gave her a big hug, smiled, and told her, "No." Feel free to treat your Crab the same way.

Romance Rating

*The only time a woman succeeds in completely
changing a man is when he's a baby.*
ACTRESS NATALIE WOOD (JULY 20)

The best thing about a Cancer girlfriend in love is that she has a huge selfless streak.

At the height of her career, rock star Deborah Harry quietly dropped out of the limelight. For approximately three years Harry minimized her public life and musical career to care for her then-lover and Blondie guitarist, Chris Stein, who had fallen ill with a rare disease. He recovered, and though their relationship ended, they have continued their musical partnership.

This is one of the best examples of your Cancer chum in love. She doesn't hesitate to put her guy first, which is one of the reasons men fall hard for her.

The worst thing that can happen to her is that, like a real Crab that hangs on to a rock while the tide washes over it, a Cancer woman can cling to a bad relationship longer than any other sign in the zodiac, including a change-hating Taurus.

She's as slow to move in love as she is when making friends. She puts her prospective boyfriend through the same little tests while she considers his strengths and weaknesses. You would think all this caution would ensure that Cancers would have a better romantic track record than the rest of us. Nope.

Her downfall is that, should her man turn out to be the worst bastard on the planet, she might not be able to bring herself either to confront or kick him out. Like Gemini, she can expect her man to read her mind. Instead of seeking resolution one way or the other by discussing the issues, your Cancer girlfriend is much more likely to go into martyr mode and start playing head games. Unlike Gemini, she's inclined to hang on no matter how bad it gets. She withdraws emotionally, or she makes herself sick with a migraine. She clings, she cries, she makes him sleep on the couch. She does everything but take action, which is contrary to her Cardinal nature. Cardinal signs often initiate change, and even Libra, who can take an eternally long time to make up her mind, will eventually make a move.

Breaking up can be so traumatic to her that she might stick it out until he dumps her. If she's married, initiating a divorce and the destruction of her home might be unthinkable. I've known Cancer women who've clung to disastrous long-term marriages, no matter how miserable they made themselves or anyone else, rather than mention the D-word. Eventually the husbands left, to everyone's relief. Theirs included, once they realized the world didn't end when the bastard walked out.

Fortunately, your average Cancer girlfriend is much more likely to end a bad relationship than to hang on for years, although she will probably stay longer than most other signs. She'll want to change course, trying first one solution, then another, until she's exhausted her supply. Only when she feels that nothing else can be done will she consider dumping the guy, and it still might take her a few more weeks, or months, to do it.

Once she does, she'll fall apart. Rush to her side and reassure her that she's made the best and only choice she could have. Tell her how you admire her and that no one else could have endured what she has for as long. Whether she's in high school or retired, and the relationship lasted two months or twenty-five years, she needs to convince herself that it wasn't her fault. Whether this is quite true or not is moot. What she's really mourning is the breakup of that emotional link, the metaphorical home that is her soul's abode. To think that she caused it will cause her endless guilt. That's the real reason she clings. Even if she drives him away, in her mind, whoever leaves first is the bad guy.

Lena Horne's quote at the beginning of this chapter is a testament to the inner strength of your Cancer girlfriend. She can carry a huge load with grace, dignity, and courage. It's also her lesson. It's *how* the load is carried that makes it either the source of her happiness or her pain.

If you're the one who's falling apart, you can't find a more loyal or compassionate friend. She'll hold your hand, invite you to her place for the weekend, or take you on a road trip to get your mind off the mess.

As are all Cardinal signs, she can be a bit competitive when it comes to guys. As a rule, she'll be totally loyal to you. So even if she likes the same cutie, if you make the first call, she'll stand aside. If you want to keep her friendship, you better be as loyal to her. This includes casual flirting with her man, for you rowdy types. There's no such thing as casual in a Cancer chum's romantic vocabulary.

Like sisters Taurus and Libra, a Cancer girlfriend can be jealous of the time you spend away from her when you're with your man. The difference is that Cancer will feel neglected if you get so absorbed in your romance that you forget to keep in touch. When that happens, she might call you. The pretext will be a friendly chat. The real reason will be to twist your head a little by telling you that she's either been ill, she's worried about her job, or some other reason designed to lay a guilt trip on you. If that happens, do be sympathetic, but don't buy into the routine. Letting her manipulate you will damage your friendship.

All of this angst is easy to avoid. Even if you are in the throes of new lust, you should always reserve some prime time for a girlfriend.

Bitch Factor

Self-destructiveness is given a really bad rap.
MUSICIAN COURTNEY LOVE (JULY 9)

Every Cancer bad girl's rotten side is linked in some way to emotional manipulation.

Poor-me Paula is the classic, pessimistic Crab. Don't ever ask her how she is, because she'll tell you in every minute detail, and nothing will be good. She's the original doom-and-gloom girl for whom the perfect job would be walking around the block with an end-of-the-world sign hung around her neck.

She's not only a slave to her moods, she wallows in them, and she expects you to put up with her. Feel sorry for her or try to help, and your reward will be a wan smile and poor excuse why your advice won't work. Nothing you can say or do will help. She doesn't want solutions. She likes being depressed. More snail than Crab, Paula slides over your good nature with a smarmy trail of emotional slime. Don't worry about ignoring this one. You're only one in a long line of temporary friends that she always chases off with her nonstop pity party.

Poor-me Paula is easy to spot because she always looks as if she's about to burst into tears. If you're unlucky enough to share cubicle space, keep your conversations restricted to business and don't make eye contact.

Head Game Girl is next on the Cancer bad-girl list. She uses any method she can think of to manipulate you. Nothing short of a trip to the hospital will stop her from trying to control your friendship. Not because she wants to be boss. Head Game Girl thrives on acting helpless.

She's the girl in your crowd who will pout if you don't compliment her dress or tear up with "worry" if you don't call her twice a day. She'll interrupt your evening to share her latest cute pet story or interrupt your surgery because she has a headache. She clings like a wet blanket and has a personality to match. This one doesn't want a pal, she wants a mommy.

She needs a caretaker. Realism is the only way to deal with this unenlightened Crab. She can't take the truth, so dish it out in liberal quantities. Tell her she's being selfish. Tell her to quit trying to run your life. Tell her to get permanently lost.

Mommie Dearest is the worst of the worst. In her, Cancer's head games reach critical mass. This Crab will work hard to worm into your inner circle. You'll probably let her, because at first she will be as nice as any Cancer girl can be. Eventually, she'll claim to be your best friend to your face while gossiping about you behind your back. She'll spread your secrets from coast to coast and rip you to shreds with her venomous tongue. Catch her in her bad behavior, and she'll pretend it was all in good fun. Only the fun is at your expense and embarrassment.

Argue with her and she'll wilt. She'll apologize. She'll bring you a gift as a peace offering. Forgive her and she'll use your back for target practice again. She's the worst, because before you found out she was such a total bitch, she probably *was* your best friend.

Once you get over the shock, you have my permission to kick her soundly in the ass.

Bondability

Sister of the soul: Taurus, Virgo, Scorpio
Inner circle: Leo, Pisces
Party pal: Gemini, Sagittarius, Aquarius
Casual chum: Aries, Cancer, Libra, Capricorn
Famous Cancer friendship: Liv Tyler and Stella McCartney (a Virgo)

Venus in Cancer

Even the most free-wheeling Sagittarius will have a definite domestic side with Venus in Cancer. Venus here produces deeply sensitive feelings and can make the most outgoing Air sign more home loving. A Cancer Venus girlfriend is also more susceptible to easily bruised feelings, although she might not show it as readily as a Cancer Sun.

This is one of the psychic placements, and your Cancer Venus chum will often be extremely intuitive, and maybe more than a bit of a mind reader. She's also likely to be interested in the spiritual arts, even if she's a pragmatic Scorpio. She has a natural talent for psychic or occult research.

Her beauty ritual is more girl-next-door than sexy siren, with subtle makeup and vitamin-enriched creams and lotions. She loves to slather on an avocado facemask and soak in a bubble bath. Even the most beauty-conscious Libra will most likely prefer tried-and-true products such as baby powder and established brand-name cosmetics. Venus in Cancer gives every Sun sign a restrained edge in fashion. The most radical Aquarius will have a few pastel or pearl-gray-colored pieces sprinkled through her wardrobe.

This position bestows a strong loyalty to friends and family. She may believe strongly in family traditions and be interested in tracing her family tree. Honesty and integrity are important to the Cancer Venus chum, which makes the most imaginative Gemini less prone to exaggeration.

Moon in Cancer

Here, the Moon is in its natural home and enhances any Sun sign with devotion, patience, and compassion. It also brings a moody, reclusive, and reserved trait to the most exuberant Fire or social Air sign.

A Cancer Moon girlfriend is usually full of contradictions because she's subject to some of the same emotional mood swings of a Cancer Sun. This girlfriend needs to set her own pace and isn't usually the party animal type.

She can sometimes expect you to read her mind and can get her feelings hurt over the smallest issue. Cancer Moons feel their way through life and have little logic or rationality. This can make the most rational Aquarius turn into an emotional mess at times, or send an already sensitive Pisces diving into bed with a migraine when the going gets tough.

The odd thing is that for all of the histrionics this position can bring, your Cancer Moon pal is tougher than she might act. This Moon is usually fiercely protective and won't hesitate to tackle any problem or rush in to rescue you. When paired with a Fire sign, this Moon can become super-aggressive.

As a friend, a Cancer Moon is possessive and a little clingy. The most cheerful Sun sign won't be above trying to lay a guilt trip on you now and then to get her way. All in all though, here the Moon is more Big Mama than Mommie Dearest, and your BFF's emotional structure will be supportive and unshakably loyal.

Your Cancer Guy Pal

He's sweet, lovable, and a little loony. Of all the men in the zodiac, your Cancer pal's personality most closely resembles that of your Cancer girlfriend.

This loyal guy is caring and will do anything for you. He's a nurturing worrier. He also likes to be nurtured and worried over. He appreciates sincerity, so don't ask him how he is unless you really want to know. He might vent his day to you, but he'll also listen if you want to vent yours.

He's the buddy to call to come over to watch a movie and share take-out. His reserved side will impress the power players at a formal event, and he'll know how to behave around your parents if you take him to a family wedding.

If he's handy, you'll never have to call a repairman, for he will insist on saving you time and money by taking care of those guy chores around your home. He'll spend the day helping you run errands or drive you to a job interview in another town.

All Cancers have moods, guys included. When he's in an emotional funk, you can get him out of it with humor. Tell him a silly joke. Or take him to a comedy flick. When you're down, he'll listen to your problems and provide sound advice for solving them.

If you have man trouble, he won't hesitate to come to your rescue. He also won't be able to resist giving you fatherly advice about the true nature of men, regardless of his age. If you're going on a first date or to a party with a new group of friends, your Cancer buddy is one guy who will keep his cell on in case you need him. He'll also analyze each of your boyfriends. None of them will probably be good enough for you. Don't worry about it; he's operating from his Big Daddy perspective. If he has girl trouble, this is one of the guys who is apt to open up to you. Don't push him for details or give him too much advice. What he really wants is to know that you're on his side.

You always will be.

Chapter Five
Leo

July 23–August 22
Element: Fire
Quality: Fixed
Symbol: The Lion
Ruler: The Sun
Birthstone: Ruby
Colors: Gold, yellow, royal purple
Flowers: Sunflower, marigold, begonia, peony
Fragrances: Orange, oriental spice, frangipani

Soul Design

Anything's possible if you've got enough nerve.
AUTHOR J. K. ROWLING (JULY 31)

Outgoing.

Bossy.

Egocentric.

These are some of the traditional descriptions of Leo. Contrary to popular astrology, however, this woman is no ego-ridden bimbo elbowing her way through life demanding all the attention. Your Leo girlfriend is generous, warmhearted, and as reliable as the sunrise once you win her loyalty.

Yes, she's definitely outgoing. Her charismatic nature is ruled by the bright, steady flame of the Sun. Even a quiet Leo chum has bursts of megawatt energy, plus the ability to grab your and everyone's attention with a not-so-subtle display of either silliness or drama. The foundation of her exuberant side is where Leo lives on the zodiac wheel. Her astrological home base is the Fifth House. Some words associated with this lively pad are *creativity, fun, sex for procreation and recreation, romance, entertainment,* and *risk taking.* This is the House of the Heart, and the Pleasure Principle, decidedly not the abode for an introverted soul.

According to the reincarnation theory, in this life, your Leo pal's soul moved here from the shy, emotion-ridden, Fourth House world of Cancer, who usually runs from the spotlight and prefers a small circle of friends. Unlike Cancer's cautious affections, which are only bestowed upon a chosen few, big-hearted Leo's love has no boundaries. In the Fifth House, the soul lets it all hang out. It seeks center stage and all the admiration and high drama that accompany the spotlight. Leos are the zodiac's superstars, and in this pad it's forever opening night.

Yes, she'll always prefer to be boss. This isn't because she arbitrarily spouts orders to make herself feel important. A Leo's inner nature is idealistic. In her heart, she's as quixotic as Pisces, envisioning a perfect life. Instead of Pisces' wish to be rescued by a fairytale hero, Leo wants to be the heroic one. Like a queen who is responsible for ruling her subjects, a Leo female feels responsible to lead even when she isn't sure where she's going. Both her motivation and her belief are that she can change things for the better. You. Herself. The world.

Think of Leo Martha Stewart. Her irritating perfectionism has become the punch line for countless late night jokes. Yet, Stewart's dedication to providing every woman with the tools to add a touch of elegance to her life is typical Leo style. Not to mention her leonine ability to rise above any hardship, self-inflicted or not. Few other signs would have demanded to go to jail and get it over with or not have lost their self-esteem while being the object of such a media circus. In the end, Stewart took command.

Leo is *Masculine Fixed Fire.* Her ruler, the Sun, is Fixed in our sky, the focal point around which all of other planets revolve. Its flame burns bright and steady. Ms. Leo's ego and emotions are also Fixed— that is, not easily changed. Your Leo chum tends to see things from a black-and-white perspective and has difficulty understanding other people's points of view. As with the other Fixed signs of earthy Taurus, watery Scorpio, and airy Aquarius, there aren't many shades of gray in a Lion's color scheme. The Masculine polarity adds to her assertiveness and to her sense of responsibility to tell you what she thinks. If you don't want an honest answer, don't ask her opinion. Her devotion to her family and circle of chums, including you, rarely wavers, too. Leo is one of the most loyal signs in the Universe.

Throughout the ages, her astrological symbol of the noble Lion has been known as the king and queen of beasts. They are regal, proud—a group of lions is called a "pride"—and fearless rulers of the jungle. It's the lioness that controls the pride. She is the huntress who provides the food and is a patient, devoted mother who nurtures her cubs.

This gregarious and fun-loving female adores being where the action is and genuinely likes people. Even Leos who are more tomboy than temptress have a natural charisma that appeals to men, women, children, and small animals. This sunny magnetism is why it's very easy to make friends with a Lioness. Talking to her is effortless because she's usually full of stories. At first, it's all about her. Don't confuse it with Aries' need to *be* first or to have the conversation center around her. Leo is checking your reactions, to see what you'll think of her. Once she feels secure, she'll want to know everything about you too. Honest flattery will open the friendship door because to her it means that you like something about her. This girl needs to be liked (even envied) despite how subtly she comes across. Make sure your compliments are genuine. A funny contradiction about Ms. Leo is that, while she's known for falling for shallow guys with pretty faces, she can spot a phony female faster than a Capricorn can sniff out a hot deal on designer duds.

Yes, she can be a show-off and drama queen. Her motivation isn't arrogance. What she really wants is to know that you're on her side. Therefore, she frequently makes a big deal out of small issues. A freak cut her off in traffic, the bitch at the office made a snooty remark, or she got a crank call on her cell. Creating drama stirs things up and keeps her in the spotlight. Inside, she craves that special recognition that makes her stand out from the crowd. If she feels she's being ignored, she won't waste time letting you know. She may trample your feelings in her rush to reclaim her space, but not with malice. No Fire sign is known for its sensitivity. Sagittarius, for instance, can win the clueless award. So, don't be afraid to make a little noise of your own if you want to keep a piece of the stage. She'll respect you for standing up for yourself.

Treat her like your favorite kitty cat, with frequent head-pats and praise, and you'll stay high on her A-list. Don't expect her to put you on speed dial if you are a quiet type who prefers watching videos and desires a mutually exclusive friendship. This girlfriend hates dead time. Sure, she can be as indolent as her jungle counterpart. But, hers is an elegant, spend-the-day-at-the-spa-being-pampered laziness versus a permanent laid-back style like that of sisters Taurus or Pisces.

Style is crucial to a Leo, and so are her looks. But this girlfriend isn't constantly checking the mirror because she's narcissistic—that's Libra's vanity. Ms. Leo is checking for flaws. Regardless of how hot she looks in a business suit or bikini, your Leo friend is always worried about her appearance. If she's on a shoestring budget, she'll scour the sale racks to put together a wardrobe that looks coordinated and more expensive than she actually paid. Even if she's a plus size, she'll seldom be sloppy. This is where those genuine compliments from you will pay off.

Another popular misconception about this fiery sign is that she's über-confident. Hardly. The real reason she devotes so much time to thinking about herself is that she's full of insecurities and a driving need to be perfect.

The worst thing you can do to a Leo is to ignore her. Maybe you forgot to ask her opinion before making an important decision, or you were excited when another friend showed up after acting tired around her. You get the picture. If she feels unappreciated, she can get gloomy in a heartbeat, and if she's gloomy, you can bet that you and everyone else will know it. If you take her for granted too long, she'll kick you out of her inner circle—with her usual flair for drama, of course.

J. K. Rowling is right. Every Lioness is nervy. She's brave and strives for perfection. She can be set in her ways and opinionated, but she's also idealistic, inspiring, and she'll stick by you through thick and thin. If you want a pal who's full of life and who can help you to bring out your best, you couldn't ask for a better friend.

Groove Meter

Grudge no expense—yield to no opposition—forget fatigue.
AMERICAN ABOLITIONIST MARIA WESTON CHAPMAN (JULY 24)

Whether she's eighteen or eighty, a hardcore party animal or home-loving pussycat, every female Leo was born to boogie. This girlfriend will find a way to snag front row tickets to the hottest concert, appear in the most outrageous outfit at a pal's summer bash, or manage to rub elbows with the richest bachelor in the room at a formal charity soiree.

She's spontaneous. You won't have to plan weeks ahead, as with a Virgo pal, because Leo's a do-it-now woman who's always ready to have fun with you at the last minute. She loves crowds and is easily enthused, which makes her a great buddy to take anywhere from a NASCAR race to the grand opening of an upscale nightclub. If you're a thrill seeker who's looking for a chum to ride roller coasters or try skydiving with, Leo's a pal to ask along.

All Leos are a little bit stagestruck. She'll be first at the mic on karaoke night at her favorite hangout. Most Leo girls love to dance and are ballsy enough to grab any hot body to groove to the music with, dirty dancing included. If there isn't a guy handy, she'll dance with her girlfriends or on a tabletop by herself.

This girlfriend was born to shop. She loves luxury as much as sister Capricorn. The difference is, whereas Ms. Cappy will save her dough and wait for that special item to go on sale, Ms. Leo can't be bothered. She wants it, now. To her, it isn't really luxurious unless it's expensive. That's why her credit card is maxed most of the time. If you want to hit the megamalls for an all-day shop-a-thon, she's another pal to call.

Most girls like surprise parties, but Leos absolutely adore them. Sure, part of the reason is that attention-getting thing. Mostly, she'll be genuinely touched because you took the time to plan something special in her honor. She's sentimental. So, if it's her birthday, save the sarcastic or satirical age-related joke cards for your Sagittarius, Taurus, or Gemini buds. You don't have to give her one that's sappy, just friendly and appreciative. She'll love bold jewelry or accessories in her favorite hot color, or anything gold colored, from a shimmery camisole to a pair of 14-carat earrings. Leo's the sign of the gambler, so lottery tickets, or a card that says you've entered her name in a drawing for a fabulous car or exotic getaway will thrill her. If it's a bridal shower, luxurious lingerie or a unique accessory for her home will please her.

Whether she's college bound or retired, forget the practical when buying gifts for your Leo pal, and give her things that add to her strong sense of style and flair for the dramatic.

Speed Bumps

You either love me or you hate me.
SINGER WHITNEY HOUSTON (AUGUST 9)

All Fire signs are outspoken. Sagittarius blurts out most everything that comes into her mind without either forethought or malice. Aries blathers her opinion regardless of whether or not you're interested or listening. Leo's conversation is sprinkled with judgment calls. This girl lives by the *Do as I say and not as I do* rule. She expects you to take her advice on everything from hairstyles to men. Don't, and you could get a lecture. She won't hesitate to say exactly how she feels at the moment. If you're going to be buddies, you'll have to learn how to verbalize your appreciation for her concern without letting her well-meant meddling permanently piss you off.

She'll try hard to conceal it, especially from her best pals, but like sister Aries, the Lioness can be one of the most jealous girls in the zodiac. Sometimes her need for attention overrides her sincerity in applauding your achievements. When she's demanding the spotlight, or shoving you out of the way to get it, you won't care about her inner motivation. You'll feel like kicking her in the ass. Of course she deserves a swift boot in the butt, and you have every right to apply it. However, as Leo is one of the most charming signs in the zodiac, about two seconds after you begin to bitch her out for her rude behavior, you're likely to find yourself on the receiving end of a full-frontal charisma attack. This is where Ms. Leo flashes you a big old toothy lion-grin, full of affection and camaraderie that totally disarms you and makes you think that you might have made an unjustified snap judgment. The key here is that you called her attention to her unfair behavior, and she's savvy enough to back off to prevent permanent damage to your friendship. She's also smart and prideful enough to manage it without an outright apology. Once the air clears, your Leo pal will forget the whole thing happened. It's good if you can forget it too, because you'll probably have to periodically repeat this scene, as she has a hard time sharing the limelight. Plus, she's so vivacious, charming, and just plain sexy that you'll sometimes feel your own green-eyed monster's angst at her.

Although she's quick to laugh at herself, *you* should never make your Leo pal the butt of a joke. Not even a harmless one that any other girl in the zodiac would think hilarious. Her pride won't stand it. She may not call you on it, but she will be wounded, and she won't forget. Plus, she wouldn't do that to you.

Her moods strike like lightning and dissipate as fast. She would rather eat a bug than be caught crying, even in front of you, so she copes by getting angry. She'll stir up a drama about some innocuous incident to hide the fact that she's hurting over something else. Some gentle questioning from you could get her to tell you the real reason she's upset, but if she chooses not to spill her guts, don't worry. As with every Fixed sign, she won't talk until she's ready, and nothing you can say or do will change that fact. Knowing that you care means everything to her.

On the other hand, if you're sobbing your heart out, she'll offer you her shoulder. She'll do anything to help you resolve any problem you have *if* she doesn't sense that you're indulging in a pity party. Leo understands deep emotions, but singing the moody blues isn't her style, and she won't tolerate it in a friend. If you want unconditional sympathy, go to your Pisces pal. Or, if you're in the mood for a communal whine-fest, seek out sisters Virgo or Cancer.

Leo is the most public of all the signs, and she won't like any violation of her rules of public behavior. The catch here is that her rules depend upon her mood of the night. If she's drunk and dancing on the table, then it's fine for you to jump up there with her. But if she's in lady mode and you get hammered and jump on the bartender, she could decide to go DQ (drama queen) and make you the incident of the night. Fortunately, your Leo pal's moods are easy to read because she *is* so dramatic.

Romance Rating

In college I castrated twenty-one rats,
and I got pretty good at it.
ACTRESS LISA KUDROW (JULY 30)

Unfortunately, Ms. Leo is not the best judge of character in the zodiac. Leos equate beauty with goodness, and even the smartest Lioness is susceptible to falling for the cute bad boy with tight abs and heartbreaker history. Snagging the eye candy everyone else wants boosts her self-esteem.

Another flaw in her ability to choose a suitable mate is that Leo is a little afraid of men she can't easily change or boss around. If he's a bit of a Weak Willie, she'll zero in and almost immediately set about trying to mold him into her ideal man. She's not dumb. She lacks an inner supply of self-confidence equal to her outer strong-woman persona. If she were to pick a man who demanded of her what she asks of herself, she would try to let him rule because she has a hard time giving up on relationships. Eventually, her need to call the shots would destroy the match. But hanging onto Willie isn't any better, because she can't respect a man who lets her boss him around.

You'll be in a race if you both spot a yummy hunk at the same time. The best thing for your friendship is to agree on an I-saw-him-first signal that allows one of you to make the first move. If that one fails to score, then the other gets her turn. If you leave it to the moment, your Leo pal will move in for the kill without thinking about you. Set the rules beforehand, and she'll honor them.

Your Leo girlfriend has too much pride to wear her heart on her sleeve, so she may act like she doesn't care that the stud she's set it on is worthless. But she does. Inside, she'll suffer, and if you're her best bud, she'll probably confess her heartbreak. You can listen, hold her hand, and nod in sympathy. You can offer nonjudgmental suggestions. But don't diss the guy. She'll take it as a putdown to her ability to choose. It's frustrating, because until she figures out that she's better off without the bastard, you'll have to slap a smile on your face when he's around to avoid hurting her.

On the other hand, if your guy is a jerk, she assumes that she knows what's best for you and won't hesitate to tell you straight out, even bluntly. She's perfectly capable of mapping out the strategy for you to leave and finding you new digs if you need them. If you're married, she'll present you with the names of the three most ball-breaking divorce attorneys in town.

No, it isn't fair. She butts in to run your life, while you have to be careful when talking about hers. However, she's operating from the Leo perspective of benevolent ruler and out of genuine loyalty and love for you. Unlike Water signs, Fire souls are not telepathic, empathetic, or subtle. Your Leo friend assumes that you want her help because, in her opinion, who wouldn't? This woman needs to be needed. Even when she's bitching about having too many people depending on her, or that her boyfriend, husband, or booty call is a helpless mess, she's secretly pleased when she's in command. She's building self-confidence points.

Bitch Factor

There are those who are marked for death.
I have my little list. . . .
SINGER JENNIFER LOPEZ (JULY 24)

A combination of pride and competitiveness is the Leo female's Achilles' heel.

The most commonly annoying behavior is that she assumes the role of Leading Lady within her inner circle, and even her best friend will have to play second fiddle. Rarely will you find a Leo who is either so introverted, or so enlightened, that she'll accept the part of bit player in any other female's entourage. Unless she's a Leading Lady, most are willing to at least share center stage with their closest chums.

The Leading Lady type of Lioness heads a clique full of girls, all who lean on her and seek her advice. While she might genuinely want to help to a degree, the prime motivation of this type of Lioness is that she can't stand competition. Competition with the Leading Lady includes rivalry for any hot body within scent-sniffing distance, even your man. She won't hesitate to flirt right in front of you or slip him her cell number when you're in the ladies room. Once he's dumped you to worship the ground she'll make him crawl on, she'll be genuinely upset should you call her out on her bad behavior. In her mind, she'll have twisted the scenario to make it all his idea, then have the balls to tell you that you both know that she's a better match for him. Fortunately, the majority of Leo females are totally loyal to their friends.

After he's dumped her for the hot little Scorpio in the corner booth, even if Ms. Leading Lady is sorry that she ruined your friendship, her pride won't allow her to apologize. If you do decide to speak to her again, even as you're sharing a glass of wine and bashing his bastard ways together, be prepared for her to assume the role of your savior. After all, didn't she expose him for the rotten loser he was, and isn't it better that you found out now than, God forbid, after you married him? Write her off, because her M.O. won't change.

Second to man stealing, idea stealing is next on Leo's list of dirty tricks. Sometimes it comes disguised as generosity, as when Ms. Helpful Coworker jumps in at the last second with assistance on a project you created that could boost you to the next rung on the corporate ladder. Not many can be as open hearted and willing to help as Leo. But, this example of support comes with an anything-to-win ulterior motive. By the time the project's wrapped and you're ready to present it to the boss, she will have begun to refer to your brainstorm as "our idea." Or worse, try to take all the credit. Usually, it's because she's not happy with her own work or needs to feed on your creativity because she's too stupid to stand out from the group herself. Understanding her motivation won't mean anything when you go ballistic over a plan you've sweated your guts out on because she's just waltzed in and tried to commandeer the project. When dealing with Ms. Helpful Coworker, make sure that everyone knows upfront that you are creator and team leader. She'll probably pull her offer of help when she realizes that she's been had, but you're better off burning the midnight oil alone than with this backstabber at your side.

Worst on Leo's bad-bitch list is Pussy Powerbroker. Tread carefully when you confront her. All Pussy P. cares about is money and power, and she'll do anything or anybody to get what she wants. This bitch won't hesitate to sleep with your man, steal your job, or lie through her teeth to make you look bad. Her queen complex is so deep seated that she plans every move before making it, and crafts every scene to give herself the maximum advantage. Pussy Powerbroker is a control freak. Instead of using Leo's charisma to get her way, she prefers to destroy anything that gets in her way. If confronted with her, call a Gemini, Scorpio, or Capricorn to help brainstorm your tactics in how to deal with her. She can be brought down, but you'll have to paint your nails Jungle Red and prepare for all-out war.

Air signs can be vindictive, Water signs vengeful, and Earth signs unforgiving. But if Fire isn't contained, either by a strong relationship or a firm direction in life, it consumes everything in its path.

Bondability

Sister of the soul: Libra, Sagittarius
Inner circle: Aries, Cancer, Virgo, Pisces
Party pal: Taurus, Gemini, Leo
Casual chum: Scorpio, Capricorn, Aquarius
Famous Leo friendship: Madonna and Gwyneth Paltrow (a Libra)

♌

Venus in Leo

Put Venus on center stage, shove a mic in her hand, and stand back. This girlfriend is wired and ready to show the world what a bombshell she can be. Venus in Leo is self-indulgent, magnetic, and theatrical. This chum could most likely earn her living in a Venus-ruled profession such as acting, music, or art.

Vanity is Venus's middle name, and the Sun is the center of our Universe. Combine the two and you have a personality trait that gives an extravagant side and flair for the dramatic to the thriftiest Virgo or most reserved Capricorn.

This girlfriend will spend any amount of money to look good and is perfectly capable of maxing out her credit card if she doesn't have the cash. She'll most likely have a cosmetics drawer to rival a Hollywood makeup artist and standing appointments with a masseuse, cosmetician, and hair stylist. Her closet will be full of the latest sleek, sexy fashions, and at least a couple of pieces of expensive jewelry.

Leo Venus is super-affectionate and fun loving. She's loyal, with the caveat that she has to think you deserve her devotion. She will expect your devotion in return and could start a small war if she feels that you are taking advantage of her in any way.

Venus here is prideful and can give an egotistical edge to the shyest Taurus or most retiring Pisces. However, it also lightens up the moodiest Sun and adds a generous, outgoing, and just plain likeable aspect to any girl's personality.

Moon in Leo

A Leo Moon brings warmth and stability to the emotional character of any Sun sign. Leo Moons are naturally optimistic and lighten the moody tendencies of even the most brooding Water sign. They are sincere, charismatic, and can be generous to a fault. They are also fanatically independent and live by their own rules.

Your Leo Moon pal usually lets her heart rule her head, and even the most logical Air sign is more likely to act on how she feels about an issue rather than looking at the facts. Like the Leo Sun, this Moon is romantic and likes to be the center of attention. However, she grabs the spotlight with charisma and humor instead of the more ego-driven antics of this Sun sign.

Most astrologers agree that Leo is one of the best signs for the Moon to occupy because of its deep and consistent emotional nature. You can depend on this girlfriend. She is loyal without being controlling, and ready to lend a hand whether you need a ride to work or help moving across the state.

This Moon bestows natural leadership qualities, and the most reclusive Pisces will be more assertive and self-directed with this placement. The Leo Moon will add creativity to the Fire signs, enhance the persuasiveness of the Air signs, boost the passion and money-making abilities of the Earth signs, and deepen the emotional magnetism of the Water signs.

Your Leo Guy Pal

You can count on a Leo buddy. Whether he's older or younger than you, he'll always assume the role of big brother. He's generous with both his time and money. He won't hesitate to buy your lunch or try to help you out of a jam. He will be interested in your love life and won't delay to tell you what he thinks of your latest boyfriend. He'll also be happy to beat him up, should the need arise.

As is Aries, the Leo is either quiet and observant, or loud and boisterous. He's not dual natured as are Gemini and Pisces. He's the human equivalent of a real Lion. Whether he's a party animal or a cat on the fireside, he's prideful and courageous. He is a tease. He'll flirt with you but not in the innuendo-laden way a Sagittarius or Gemini would. He's more into kidding you about a crush you have on another guy or vice versa.

He's another social dude whom you can take anywhere. He won't leave your side during the evening, partly because he has an old-fashioned sense of chivalry about him and partly because he's keeping one eye on you while sizing up any other males that may be heading your way. This doesn't mean he'll prevent you from having fun. He's vetting the possibilities, and he has good instincts. Your girlfriends will probably fall for him because of his natural charisma, and he'll love charming them. He's a man who can make every woman feel beautiful and every other guy want to copy his style.

Be sure always to thank him for every good deed he does. He's funny about it. He'll go out of his way to help you and won't expect reciprocation. But he does expect your thanks. Considering that he's idealistic, honest, loyal, and willing to defend you as if he were your real brother, that's not asking much.

Chapter Six
Virgo

August 23–September 22
Element: Earth
Quality: Mutable
Symbol: The Virgin
Ruler: Mercury
Birthstone: Sapphire
Colors: Shades of beige and brown, bright green
Flowers: Morning glory, narcissus, pansy
Fragrances: Apple, lemongrass, chamomile, coconut

Soul Design

I can spend hours in a grocery store . . .
arranging my baskets so everything fits in and
nothing gets squashed. I'm really anal about it, actually.
ACTRESS CAMERON DIAZ (AUGUST 30)

Sweet.

Reserved.

Nitpicky.

Remember watching ants when you were a kid? Those perpetually busy little creatures were always carrying ten times their weight and never stopped to rest. Your Virgo girlfriend is like that; she always has a lengthy to-do list and is rarely without her daily planner. Yes, she strives to always do her best. No, she is absolutely not the humorless nitpicker as some astrology books portray her. Winning her casual friendship is easy, as she is a social creature. But if you think getting elevated to her BFF status takes two things—never be late and always be tidy—you're wrong. Common astrology is full of misconceptions about your Virgo friend. These are two more.

Another is her perfectionist label. A better word for her nature is *discriminating*. Yes, she wants things to be just right, and in order to do that, she'll pick and choose, weigh and consider the options, until she's come up with a mix that suits her style, her taste, or her whim of the moment. Whether that's a graciously appointed home filled with exquisite furnishings or a comfortable jumble of dust-covered clutter, she'll feel at home in each. It's her search for the right fit, not the perfect-world idealism of sisters Aquarius and Pisces.

She's *Feminine Mutable Earth*. Her Earth nature makes her as concerned with security and stability as are sisters Taurus and Capricorn. Her Mutable perspective makes her more flexible than either the Bull or the Goat. Her Feminine side gives her a natural empathy.

The Virgo soul lives in the Sixth House of Work, Service, and Health. Associations here are helpfulness to others, especially those with whom she works, and concern with health issues. In leaving the playful Fifth House, the soul buckles down to concentrate on the work of the day job. It also struggles to achieve self-discipline in health and life, and it makes do with what it has at hand.

As is sister Gemini, your Virgo girlfriend is ruled by sociable, chatty Mercury, the Winged Messenger god who rushed around the heavens bearing the latest news and gossip. The caveat with the Virgin is that, in Earth, Mercury's wings are somewhat clipped. Your Virgo friend might be the chattiest of the Earth signs, and very social. However, she is far less outgoing or changeable than Gemini. The Virgin internalizes much of her Mercurial nature. Her practical Earth wants to contain Mercury's impulsive nature.

She's as questioning as Gemini, but a Virgo chum's questions stem from her cautious nature and manifest as a check and double check to make sure everything is safe or correct. "Are you sure?" "Did you turn off the iron?" "Did you remember to check the air in the tires?" This is how she earned her reputation as the zodiac nitpicker. Yes, it can make you want to scream. She's neither trying to prove you wrong nor does she feel superior by proving herself right. Mercury says, "Don't sweat the small stuff. You're overreacting." Her practical Earth says, "How irresponsible. I could never have fun worrying whether the house will burn down or we'll have a blowout and wreck the car."

Her rule in life is to get the facts, then *proceed with caution*. Understanding that this is her basic soul design will help you to keep from clenching your jaws when you're around your Virgo pal. You could also be grateful that she is so conscientious. Especially if you are an impulsive Fire sign or sometimes scattered Cancer or Pisces.

I had a Virgo friend who always had a checklist of things to remember whenever our crew went on a road trip. She thought of everything from servicing the car to who brought what snacks, and she kept the rest of us organized. At first her preoccupation with the details was a running joke. Soon we depended on her planning skill to keep us on track and on time. She likes to be needed, but in a useful way. Showing that you appreciate her sensible side will keep you close to this often misunderstood woman.

So will respecting her privacy. She's not into prying into your life, and one way to win her friendship is to not pry into hers. Like Scorpio, she guards her personal life. The difference is that if she has a problem and you're close to her, she's much more likely to confide in you. She's not the type for tearful displays in front of your inner circle, though, so don't expect a public pity party from this girlfriend.

Her symbol, the Virgin, has also been misconstrued through the ages. This dilution of the original character has resulted in the popular astrology version of her as repressed or cold natured. Virgo is the goddess who sustained life on Earth, and she did it alone. She had no husband but consorted with anyone she chose. She wasn't only sexy; she had a free-love attitude thousands of years before the hippie generation existed.

When you put the Virgin sustainer of life into the Sixth House of Work, Service, and Health, it's easier to understand why she's constantly assessing issues, gathering the facts, and dispensing her opinions on how to make things better. Or why some of your Virgo friends seem to be preoccupied with health. Sustaining life takes proper nourishment and exercise.

Your Virgo girlfriend might seem cool on the surface, but she's full of nervous energy. This can turn her into as much of a verbal hurricane as either a Gemini or Sagittarius chum in high gear. Her conversation is aimed at giving you all the details. This can cause her to chatter for an hour about her trip to the mall when all you want to know is whether she found the outfit she wanted. She'll tell you the entire plot of the book she's just read or give you a blow-by-blow description of the run-in between two of her coworkers, and her analysis of why they had the fight. This is Mercury's need to communicate. The exasperating part is that unlike Gemini, who chatters about lots of topics with little detail, Virgo painstakingly gives you *every* detail.

Her attention to details extends beyond filling you in on everyday minutiae. Her discriminating nature leads to a meticulous attitude toward whatever she tries to do, and she usually develops an admirable skill at whatever she attempts. She learns by being patient, doing and undoing until she learns the craft, the art, or her everyday work from the inside out.

This attention to detail can also work against her. A Virgo girl-friend can get so caught up in the details that she falls behind on the project, or the artwork never gets finished, or she simply gets over-whelmed.

When that happens, offer to help. She'll appreciate it because you're being helpful instead of only empathizing. Grin and bear it when she hands over part of the project, for even if it's something you thoroughly understand, she's compelled to give you a lesson. Plus, she'll frequently check to see if you're doing it her way.

She's thrifty. Your Virgo girlfriend is as good at spotting bargains as Taurus. The difference is that Taurus looks for value at the lowest price in order to acquire as many things a possible on her budget. Every Virgo was born with the innate fear of starving. No matter how well off she gets in life, she'll always worry about losing everything. She looks for values so that she will always have what she needs, and some money left over for that proverbial rainy day. This is one girl-friend who'll get up at 4 A.M. to be first in the door with you at a Black Friday sale.

She can be obsessive. This is the trait that is often confused as per-fectionism. Her earthy soul needs to control the undisciplined energy of Mercury. Whether she goes so far as to arrange her pantry accord-ing to food groups or separate her towels according to color groups, or always uses her red cup for coffee and her green one for tea, this girlfriend will probably be a slave to some sort of ritual. Nothing is black and white to your Virgo chum. At a restaurant, she's the friend who picks apart the menu to mix and match the dinner selections to suit her taste. She'll ask her hairstylist to snip an eighth of an inch more off her bangs. No more, no less. She blends and fuses and inte-grates until she's comfortable. Then she sticks to the ritual.

While some Virgos are certain to be neat freaks, this is another myth that stems from the perfectionist assumption. She can be as much of a junk collector as the rest of us. Her need for order is internal, not external. Her rituals are her safety net when her world gets chaotic.

A Virgo girlfriend isn't into running your life as a Cardinal sign would, or forcing her opinions on you as a Fixed sign might. She's into tweaking things for you. She'll show you the rainbow of options between white and black that you can tap into make life easier, more productive, and just right for you.

Groove Meter

I'm more private than people realize.
I'm not that easy to get to know.
SINGER SHANIA TWAIN (AUGUST 28)

She's not the most spontaneous sign in the zodiac, so the first rule of partying with your Virgo chum is to plan ahead. If you want to go to the movies on Friday night, call her Tuesday. If it's a weekend out of town, give her a week or two's notice.

As we all do, your Virgo pal has a party hardy side. She can dance the night away with the best Sagittarius, or flirt up any guy with the coyest Libra. It's how she handles the evening, the guy, and herself that sets her apart. Usually, if she drinks too much, she'll ask to be taken home. She might dance all night, but not on top of the bar. She might have a deluge of guys asking for her number, but she won't be fawning or hanging on any of them. I don't think I've ever seen one of my Virgo friends totally out of control. That doesn't mean that it never happens, but I've never witnessed it.

A Virgo girlfriend is neither aloof nor snobbish. Keeping the flirting light, the drinking in moderation, the fun at a certain level are rituals designed to help keep order in her outer world, the same as she tries to do in her inner one.

As the other Earth signs, your Virgo pal loves the outdoors. She'll probably have a vegetable garden or is a nature lover into camping. If you're into hiking or biking along scenic trails, she's the chum to take along. Suggest a game of tennis or badminton. Most Virgos like sports, but she's more into one-on-one for fun than a serious competitor, although she likes cheering in person for her favorite team. A Virgo chum also like puzzles, chess, or other board games that challenge her mind.

She's another girlfriend who can pull together a designer-chic look on a shoestring budget. Ask for her help when you're shopping for the perfect look. She'll take you everywhere from a major department store to the local gently used clothing shop, selecting a sweater here and shoes there, mixing and matching the right textures, shades, and styles until it's totally right and totally you.

Want a friend to peruse the used bookstore with? Call her. She's usually an avid reader and will love getting more for her money. She can spend hours at a flea market, antique mall, or street fair, picking out complementing accessories for her home. This girl is resourceful. She can refinish her own furniture or help you paint your kitchen, do minor repairs around the house, and even change the oil in her car. Don't think she's too prissy to get her hands dirty. She's down to earth, realistic, and knows that if you want something done right, learn how to do it yourself.

Be a good sport if her idea of dinner and drinks is a vegetable juice cocktail at the local salad bar because she's trying out a vegan diet. It's her soul's pattern to be concerned with her health. Even if she's a plus size, she'll be into vitamins or working on a diet or trying to exercise. You can help her by steering her to a good nutritionist or encouraging her to keep trying. She's a great gym partner. Regular workouts appeal to her. So do aerobics.

When planning a party in her honor, whether it's a casual backyard picnic or a black tie event, think of simplicity. Pretty decorations, fresh flowers on the table; understated elegance versus streamers, banners, and a ceiling full of balloons. More is definitely not better with your Virgo friend. With her penchant for planning ahead, a surprise party might not be the best choice for this chum.

She's also not really into gag gifts. She'll laugh at them, but this girlfriend prefers something useful. That can be anything from a personal journal to a diamond watch. She'll love clean-smelling soaps or citrus-scented lotions and bath products. A gift card to her favorite book or cosmetics store will make her happy. Books or a subscription to her favorite magazine are always reliable choices. So is a gift certificate to a health food store.

If you're planning her bridal shower, she'll prefer gift selections from her bridal registry, like her sister Taurus. She'll also love anything that complements her taste. Be sure to include an exchange receipt, because Virgo girls have no guilt about exchanging items that don't quite fit. A gift card for the lingerie shop is a good idea, as she will want to try on everything until she looks perfect.

Speed Bumps

Good advice is always certain to be ignored,
but that's no reason not to give it.
NOVELIST AGATHA CHRISTIE (SEPTEMBER 15)

"No." "I told you so." "It won't work." Anyone who has a Virgo girlfriend has heard these lines or some version of them many times. It's one of her most exasperating traits and the reason she's earned the nitpicker label. She doesn't intend her criticisms as negative, or to make you feel inferior. She can't help herself. She's operating from her soul's need to check, recheck, and find the best way.

Understanding her soul's perspective on fine-tuning life can help you to realize that her observations and criticisms aren't meant as barbs, but to be helpful. That might prevent you from losing your cool when your head is buzzing from listening to her. When she's on a roll, this girl can expound until your eyes cross.

Her need to plan ahead can be a big pain in the butt, especially when you've snagged last-minute tickets to a play or the gang is getting together on the spur of the moment. She may or may not decide that she can join you. You ask. She answers, "Let me see if I can make it. I'll call you back." Then you fume about having to wait for her to make up her mind. Unfair? Seems like it until you remember that her Mercury side wants to jump at the offer and her Saturn side reminds her of all the chores she has to do tonight. She needs time to sort it out internally. It's perfectly fine for you to set a deadline so that you still have time to ask another friend. She understands that concept.

She can be obsessed with her health. Virgos all have a bit of the hypochondriac in them. She'll convince herself that she has the disease of the month as seen on the surgery channel or fuss over your eating habits until you lose your appetite. Her astrological rep for being a clean freak stems from her Sixth House connection of health through hygiene. Push this to the extreme and she can become germ phobic. Look on the bright side. Her home may be cluttered, but it's highly unlikely that you'll find anything green growing in this pal's fridge.

A Virgo girlfriend can be a walking pharmacy. I have a close Virgo friend who never travels without one of those miniature duffel bags stuffed with over-the-counter remedies. This pharmacopoeia contains hand sanitizer, sunscreen, pills from aspirin to antacids, cold remedies, sleep aids, assorted vitamins, antibiotic ointment, bandages, peroxide, and more. She's prepared for anything. Even though our crew kids her about rattling when she walks, we all admit that it's strangely comforting to know that if one of us gets a headache or bellyache in the night, she'll have something to soothe us. It's like traveling with a personal physician. Your Virgo chum might not be as excessive, and mine's had years of practice. But, even the youngest Virgo you know will probably have a well-stocked medicine cabinet.

She prides herself on controlling her emotions. In Virgo this can result in a girl who is so unspontaneous that she'll weigh the pros and cons of getting angry versus just letting go. Then she makes herself physically sick with worry. When that happens, the kindest thing you can do is take her green tea and vegetable soup or her favorite equivalent of that combination. When she's better, take her for a day trip or long ride in the country, as being outside helps to clear her head.

Her Earth nature is shy; her Mercury nature is outgoing and analytical. Instead of externalizing her emotions, she internalizes them. Bottle them up too long and you have an irritable nail biter with chronic acid stomach on your hands.

Romance Rating

I've stolen a couple of hearts
and they are in my private collection.
ACTRESS SALMA HAYEK (SEPTEMBER 2)

Regardless of how cool, shy, or aloof she may appear on the outside, inside every Virgo girlfriend is a sexy, earthy woman. Forget those tired descriptions of her as the fussy old maid, passionless ice queen, or repulsed by sex because it's vulgar and messy. Not sexy? Don't tell Salma Hayek, Cameron Diaz, or Sophia Loren.

She's a realist. One of her best traits is that she usually doesn't go into love with blinders on, as many of us do. I'm not talking about spring flings and semi-casual encounters, which Virgo girls are as prone to as the rest of us. When she does fall, it's usually with her eyes (mostly) open. She thinks that she understands his flaws and accepts them. This can lead to her downfall.

A Virgin sees what she perceives to be her man's potential, then once she's committed herself to the relationship she sets about tweaking him until *he* realizes it. Whether the guy wants to be tweaked into a better human being is a moot point. She'll redo his wardrobe because he looks better in blue than brown. She'll put him on a diet to help him lose a few pounds. She'll put him on a budget, or better for her, an allowance so they'll have money in their old age. Maybe he is a diamond in the rough. What she doesn't consider is why hasn't he done something about it himself? Simple. That's what he needs her for. Your Virgo girlfriend never feels more useful than when she's chipping the edges off a slob, trying to turn him into her hero. A Virgo woman can tweak, correct, and nudge herself right out of a relationship. Unfortunately, as do the Water girls and sister Taurus, she can hang on too long.

She tries to make do with what she has. So he's a bit of a jerk, or he's fallen off the fidelity wagon once or twice. So what? Your Virgo girlfriend will try to make the best of the situation. Instead, she'll get sick. She has vague aches and pains or a real ulcer or other digestive problems. What she won't do is face the fact that she can't make either him or the relationship better. Eventually, her nudging turns into full-blown criticizing, which makes him act worse, and the downward spiral begins.

When it finally blows apart she'll try to make the best of her heartbreak too. She'll want to be left alone at first. Respect her, but keep in touch on the phone and don't let her sit by herself too long. Your Virgo pal can indulge in a pity party of endless analyzing where she, he, they went wrong and what she could, should, or might have done differently to make things better. Buy her lunch at her favorite restaurant and take your car. She needs to be cared for too, even though she's often the strong one for everyone else.

Should she and her guy kiss and make up, she expects you to respect her decision as she would if it were you. Although she's a Mutable sign, if you point out what a jerk he is, she will have as hard a time accepting your advice as would any Fixed sign. The best thing for you to do is to act like you're happy to see him when they're together, for her sake.

She'll be totally devoted when you hurt. She'll do everything for you that I just described. Plus, she'll come and sit quietly with you at home and let you talk it out if you feel like it, or simply keep you company if you don't. She'll make her assessment of it and give you advice about what you should do next, such as taking a trip to get your mind off it, or now might be a good time to redo your bathroom. She's all for second chances. So if you give your ex one, she'll be happy for you. She'll also be on alert for any lapses from him, which she'll point out should they happen. Take her advice or not, the point is that she means well.

It's a rare Virgo friend who will even think of pushing you out of the way to get to a guy first. Her friendship bonds are strong, and she doesn't feel the need to compete.

Bitch Factor

No matter how cynical you get,
it's impossible to keep up.
COMEDIENNE LILY TOMLIN (SEPTEMBER 1)

Your Virgo girlfriend's strengths are her discriminating tastes and attention to detail; these are her weaknesses too.

The Trivia Queen pushes the need for attention to the details into the twilight zone. Sit down for a chat with this girl and soon you'll feel like that line of busy ants I mentioned earlier is crawling through your brain. Queen T. not only sweats the small stuff, she's obsessed with it. Never ask her how she is; she'll tell you. Everything—from the time her eyes opened that morning. You'll hear what song was on the clock radio, with a digression to how it reminded her of an adventure she had, and that detail as well. She'll tell you what she had for breakfast, with a sidebar on the merits of her latest diet. If she's a coworker, she'll add her commute, complete with traffic and weather reports. As it's nearly impossible to shut this one up, pretend your cell's vibrating with an important call. She'll walk away . . . still jabbering.

The Critic notices your every flaw and takes great delight in pointing out each one, both to you and everyone else you know. She'll tell you when you have a run in your nylon and that a blemish is popping up on your forehead. As if you didn't know. She'll correct your grammar in front of the boss, or wait until you're at the bar, flirting with a cutie, to announce that you have a piece of lettuce stuck in your teeth. All said with a smile, all under the pretence of doing it for your own good.

This pretend friend's brand of support is all passive aggression. She acts as if she has your best interests at heart. What she's really doing is venting her jealousy by trying to make you look bad because she doesn't have the guts to be a straightforward bitch. Don't let that stop you. Tell Ms. Critic to take her help and shove it.

By far the worst of the Virgo bad girls is Know-it-all Kate. Whatever you try to discuss with this one, she's either been-there-done-it, knows a better way to do it, or wouldn't waste her time on it. Kate is an expert on everything from men to religion, and anything you say, do, or try can't possibly be important. Make a mistake and she'll say she told you so, loud and clear, in front of anyone nearby. She's never wrong. No one else is ever right.

Kate's sole purpose is to control her inner circle by undermining everyone else's confidence until they don't trust their own judgment. Trust mine on this one, and don't waste time in kicking her out of your club.

Bondability

Sister of the Soul: Taurus, Virgo, Capricorn
Inner circle: Cancer, Libra, Leo, Scorpio
Party pal: Aries, Aquarius
Casual chum: Gemini, Sagittarius, Pisces
Famous Virgo friendship: Faith Hill and Martina McBride (a Leo)

♍

Venus in Virgo

Here, Venus can be hard to get to know. Every Sun sign will have a cautious edge to her personality when it comes to any emotional investment, whether in friendship or love. Virgo Venus has a shy charm and a tendency to analyze your pal potential and weigh any perceived faults against your virtues.

In astrology, Venus in Virgo is said to be in its *fall*. This means that your Virgo Venus chum's emotions can be so discriminating they become critical. This isn't all bad, because this is her natural defense mechanism for protecting her super-shy emotions.

She's also likely to have an air of nervous tension or anxiety about her. The most laid-back Taurus or carefree Sagittarius will be fussier and tend to worry about what you think about her. Even the headstrong Fire signs or a self-assured Capricorn can have a natural fear of making waves.

Her fashion sense is youthful and comfortable. Venus Virgo bestows a natural talent for finding the best value in anything, from a business power suit that's both classic and feminine to the perfect little black dress.

A Virgo Venus girlfriend's beauty ritual is based on health from within. She's prone to taking youth-renewing vitamins and potions and is fastidious about sticking to her daily regimen. That's why your Virgo Venus pal can seem ageless, no matter how many birthdays she's had.

She might prefer naturally made or mineral-based cosmetics minus chemicals and perfumes. This chum is another girlfriend who usually prefers subtle makeup, or nothing but a bit of mascara and a softly colored lip gloss.

Virgo Venus adds humility to the Sun sign character and bestows a talent for healing. This girlfriend has the potential to do just about anything she sets her mind to, from the medical or veterinarian professions to landscape artist to playwright.

Moon in Virgo

No matter what her Sun sign is, a Virgo Moon girlfriend's emotions are serious, analytical, and judgmental. Her inner critic can lessen the self-confidence of even the most ego-driven Leo or self-assured Capricorn. Logical and reliable, a Virgo Moon chum has a high set of standards that can either fuel her success or add a condescending aspect to her emotional makeup.

A Virgo Moon chum can be a challenge because of her instinctive need to criticize just about everything under the Sun. She can't help it. Here the emotional character becomes fussy and preoccupied with tweaking her relationships. This placement can be more nitpicky than a Virgo Sun.

She can also have trouble relaxing and suffer from frequent bouts of nervous indigestion due to her perfectionist nature. However, despite these difficulties, as a friend she's loyal and kind with a humane nature that favors the underdog. This thoughtful Moon considers every side of an issue and loves to work all the angles until she finds the best solution. A Virgo Moon girl is frequently handy at DIY projects and small home repairs. She can come up with some pretty ingenious ways to save time and money.

This Moon child is also intellectual, responsible, and hard working. A Virgo Moon anchors the flighty Air signs and curbs the reckless impulses of the Fire signs. It strengthens the determination of the Earth signs and adds a realistic outlook to the emotional Water signs.

Your Virgo Guy Pal

Whether he rides a Harley or wears a three-piece suit, this guy is as good hearted as they come. Want a buddy who'll help you weigh all the angles? He's your pal. He'll pick you up if your car breaks down or come over and play handyman. He'll make time for lunch or to hang out with you if you need some quiet time.

Stay close to this buddy by respecting his privacy by calling first if you want to see him. And ask his advice about anything from his choice of restaurants to issues at work. He'll appreciate that you value his judgment.

If you're down, he'll always try to cheer you up, usually with a series of jokes that range from plain silly to slightly naughty. His sense of humor can get a little rowdy, so don't hesitate to slam dunk him if he gets too cheeky.

Take him anywhere you want to have fun. He'll shake up a stuffy event with his wicked one-liners or flirt nonstop with your girlfriends at the local watering hole. He'll flirt with you too. Go ahead and kid him back. It's his nature and it's safe. His famous shyness only truly applies to his love life. Practicing his schmoozing side on you is a safety net for him.

He's as chatty as any of your girlfriends and will talk about any subject under the Sun, except his private life. He'll listen to you if you're having guy trouble and be there if you get your heart broken. About the only thing he'll say about himself is that everything's fine. That or he'll crack a few jokes and change the subject.

A Virgo buddy is rather like a St. Bernard—cuddly, friendly, and sometimes, goofy. He's loyal, kind hearted, and will do anything to help you out of a jam. He's one of the sweethearts of the zodiac. Consider yourself lucky that he's your friend.

Chapter Seven
Libra

September 23–October 22
Element: Air
Quality: Cardinal
Symbol: The Scales
Ruler: Venus
Birthstone: Opal
Colors: Blue, lavender, cream, and pale yellow
Flowers: Hydrangea, forget-me-not, dahlia
Fragrances: Rose, violet, honeysuckle, lemon

Soul Design

Many people will walk in and out of your life,
but only true friends will leave footprints on your heart.
FIRST LADY ELEANOR ROOSEVELT (OCTOBER 11)

Fair minded.

Indecisive.

Vain.

Your Libra friend is ruled by Venus, as is sister Taurus. In Taurus, Venus loves comfort, security, and possessions. In Libra, Venus loves the comfort and security of relationships.

It's easy to make friends with this outgoing and sensitive woman. Sociable and sweet, this girlfriend was born to bond and thrives on the energy generated by her friendships. She'll have a large circle of chums and try to divide her time equally among them.

She's *Masculine Cardinal Air;* subtle, initiating, intellectual. Libra's Masculine character is assertive but tempered by her Venus-ruled nature. She's the girl who will use honey versus a hammer to get her way. Her Cardinal trait of initiating change is focused on guiding change within her relationships. Her Air nature is generally quieter and more diplomatic that those of sisters Gemini and Aquarius.

In astrology, her intellectual side is often overlooked in favor of focusing on her Venus traits. However, this girl is usually smart, well organized, and on top of both her life and her career. It's another reason her opinion is so sought after. She has an uncanny knack for unraveling the most complex issues in an amazingly short time.

A Libra girlfriend's soul lives in the Seventh House of Partnerships and Marriage. On a personal level, it refers to the spouse or lover. It also covers partnerships related to work, business deals, contracts, or any area of human interaction. The Seventh House is all about getting along with others, including friends. Having moved here from the all-business Sixth House of Work, Service, and Health, the soul loses the obsessions of ritual-ridden Virgo and puts on its dancing shoes. It turns off the desk lamp, lights the candles, and breaks open the champagne. The key word here is *we.*

Her symbol is the Scales, the only inanimate object on the zodiac wheel. The key word associated with the Scales is *balance.* They strive to maintain equilibrium without prejudice or emotion. A Libra friend is analytical, rational, and fair, most of the time.

She's another chum who doesn't like to spend time alone, like sister Gemini. Gemini gets bored. Libra gets lonely. To create balance in her life she needs other people. A Libra girl is happiest when she has company, and her favorite communication style is face to face.

My best Libra friend and I have known each other since childhood. As we now live in different towns, we made a pact to visit at least once a month, which proved impossible with both of our busy schedules. So we visit when we can, and the rest of the time we stay in touch through frequent, sometimes daily, emails. I don't mind communicating via email. It's convenient, and, to me, less interruptive than stopping to pick up the phone. Yet, every couple weeks, if I don't call her, she'll call me and say, "I miss hearing your voice."

Your Libra girlfriend feels the same way. There aren't many things she likes better than to get together and chat. Phone chats are second. Email or text messaging comes last. Without another person physically present, your Libra chum can feel out of sorts. This girl doesn't voluntarily do solitude. You can keep her close with simple things such as having morning coffee or inviting her to ride along when you're running errands.

She's fair minded. If she gets to choose where she wants to go tonight, then she'll be sure to let you have your turn next week. You might not care who bought coffee last, but she will. She's not keeping track of you. She's keeping track of herself. It's important to her to reciprocate the gesture, the generosity, the compliment. It's not in her nature to take advantage of a person or situation. This is one girl to whom you can lend your car, your money, or your home for the weekend. She'll return the car with an equal amount of gas, be sure to repay the loan, and clean up after herself when she leaves. Other girlfriends will also do these things. However, with your Libra chum it can become a friendly obsession. Make sure to treat her just as fairly if you want to stay high on her best-friend list.

She's a champ at small talk and can single-handedly keep any conversation going for hours. She's a great listener and has the ability to make everyone around her feel important, including you. The topics of conversation won't matter. She's as interested in your career or the latest current events as she is your personal life. She's one friend that you can vent to for hours when things are going wrong. She's patient and willing to hear you out. She'll also interject thoughtful questions or remarks. Libra women often have a soothing quality to their voices that helps the rest of us to calm down.

A Libra girl loves to dress up, which makes her fun to shop with when you're after something glamorous for a formal event. She has an eye for form and color and can help you to pick the perfect outfit to complement your shape, size, and eyes. You'll have to keep an eye on your budget; she won't. She's not the thriftiest girl on Earth. She's out to find beauty, no matter what it costs.

She thrives on praise. This is a combination of having inherited both Venus's and her Seventh House's need for partnering. She's sensitive about what you might think of her, including her style. You'll rarely see her running around town in tattered jeans and a frayed tee. If you do, it's probably because she has a crisis on her hands. A Libra girl is acutely aware of her appearance and always tries to look her best, even if she's only going to the ATM after dark.

Every girl loves a compliment. Libra needs them to reassure herself that she isn't over- or underdoing anything that will embarrass either her or you. She's not into extremes in any part of life. She's also not above fishing for flattery. If you overlook her new handbag, she'll ask you what you think. You don't have to gush, but try to make a positive comment. She needs your approval that her choice was the correct one.

Yes, she can have a hard time making up her mind. Mostly it's when she's deciding what to wear or whether she wants to buy the yellow blouse or the blue one or other personal things that affect her looks and style. However, one of her more annoying habits is when you ask her to choose where to go on an outing, and she vacillates and ponders and thinks about it and never makes a decision. Before you get exasperated, stamp your foot and demand that she choose (right now!), understand that her behavior has nothing to do with being indecisive. It has nothing to do with seeking balance or playing fair or ensuring that you both have an equally great time. Secretly, she doesn't *want* to decide. Partnership-oriented Libra friends need to receive as much looking after as they give, but have a hard time asking. You pick. She'll be happy because she knows you're happy. She'll also be relieved.

The old saying, *Make the best of a bad situation,* could be her motto, for your Libra pal will always try to see both sides of any problem. She seldom loses her temper. That's why she often is the group mediator. Along with Pisces, she has a natural ability to listen without judging and will genuinely try to help resolve any rifts that pop up within her social circle.

Whether she's a teenager or a grandmother, this need to please can send her to places that she'd really rather not be. This girlfriend finds it hard to say, "No." That's why your Libra chum is often caught in the middle of everything from office wars to family feuds. She's a born diplomat, which makes her the first person that everyone goes to for advice. Her Cardinal need to lead coupled with her idealistic view of a perfectly balanced world makes her assume that she can solve everyone's problems. This sets her up to be the person with whom everyone is angry. It's always a surprise to a Libra woman when people disagree with her solutions. She strives for an equal division, where everyone gets a fair share of the responsibility, the reward, or the inheritance. Her rational, analytical Scales have taken into account all but one thing. Humans are emotional, irrational, subjective beings, especially when they are having a rift.

Your Libra girlfriend works hard to keep her own emotions in check. This is how her soul feels that the world should work, and she's right. So she's genuinely upset and a little confused when her efforts not only aren't fruitful, they get her into trouble with the people she was trying to help.

This is where you can help her. First, applaud her effort. Remember, this girl needs approval. Then gently remind her that keeping everyone else happy isn't the most important thing in life. Plus, it's impossible. She will never completely understand this fact because of her soul design. But, with your assistance, she can lessen her need to assume responsibility for making everything run smoothly and quit beating herself up when it doesn't.

Your Libra pal is never happier than when she's hanging with you. She knows how to make you feel important, cared for, and good about yourself. She's all about fair play and giving as much as she receives. You couldn't ask for a more faithful friend.

Groove Meter

If you rest, you rust.
FIRST LADY OF THE AMERICAN THEATER
HELEN HAYES (OCTOBER 10)

She's one of the social butterflies of the zodiac, and vies with Leo and Sagittarius for the hostess-of-the-year award. These two Fire signs lean toward big bashes with lots of noisy friends all laughing and talking at once. Your Libra chum is more into intimate dinners or cocktail parties where the music plays softly in the background.

It's not that she can't boogie the night away at the hottest club or drink until dawn with the best of her rowdy friends. She enjoys getting down as much as the next girlfriend. It's that her preference is often for quieter venues where everyone can chat without shouting at each other over the din.

Libra girlfriends are fun oriented, but not quite as daring as a Fire sign jumping out of an airplane or an Earth sign hiking through the wilderness. She'll like a girls' night in, munching snacks and watching her favorite movies. No matter what her age, she will probably enjoy the classic black-and-white romantic comedies or lush musicals of the '40s and '50s. She's the friend to take to the philharmonic, any formal charity or art event, and to the *Nutcracker* during the holidays.

Want to go horseback riding? Ask her. Many Libra girls love horses. She'll also enjoy watching a polo match, a dressage event, or the rodeo. She's not much for sweating it out in the gym. However, stretching-type exercise such as yoga, or even ballet lessons, will appeal to her.

Your Libra girlfriend loves to have you over for dinner, or to spend a quiet evening at her home flipping through the latest fashion magazine and gossiping about guys.

She's another girl you can include on a road trip. She'll do her share of the driving and have fun no matter where you head. I don't think there's a Libra alive who doesn't love to dance. She's into learning new dance steps, either by taking formal lessons or getting together with you and your girl crew at someone's pad to practice.

Want to redecorate your room or your house? She will love searching through fabric swatches and wallpaper albums until you find the perfect match of colors. She'll go with you to look at furniture and accessories. Your Libra chum has an eye for blending styles and picking the perfect accessories to complement your taste.

She's not as bold about it as sister Leo, but your Libra BFF adores being the center of attention too. She's not into surprise parties because she wants time to get her glam on, so it's best to let this girlfriend know beforehand. All you need to tell her is when and that you'll pick her up. The rest of the details can be a secret.

Invite all of her friends and make it as luxurious as you can. If it's a backyard bash, cover the tables with paper tablecloths in her favorite color and centerpieces of either silk or fresh flowers. If it's at a restaurant, reserve a private room where nothing will interrupt her celebration. Plan for a long evening, because she'll want to spend time with each of her friends and dance until the wee hours. If you can afford a live band, that's fine. Otherwise a portable CD or music player loaded with her favorite tunes is great.

Think luxury or whimsy versus practical gifts for both her birthday and wedding. Whatever you choose, wrap it beautifully and she'll appreciate it even more.

She loves jewelry and will like anything from an inexpensive pair of beaded earrings that match her eyes to a unique antique pin. Give her a pair of tickets to a play, a movie, or art exhibition. Get her a purse-sized version of her favorite perfume and tuck an array of fragrance samples in the gift bag as well. She likes to try new scents.

For her home, try satin, beaded, or velvet pillows for a chair or her bed. She'll love a gift card to the local art gallery. A pair of candlesticks or an unusual lamp that matches her decorating scheme are good choices. She'll like luxurious bath sheets and rose-scented bath oil, or his-and-hers matching spa robes.

A Libra girl has a wide range of tastes in lingerie. Yours could like anything from naughty to prim. If it's naughty, she'll love a gift card from an adult boutique so that she can shop with her man. If it's prim, make it white satin or pale blue silk. The key is to know her taste and follow it, as she's not as flexible as some of your other girlfriends in this area.

She can go from the rodeo to the symphony all in the same day. And will have fun whether you're heading to Acapulco for the weekend or hanging out at your pad watching TV. Affectionate, warmhearted, and sentimental, your Libra girlfriend is just the right combination of refined and rowdy.

Speed Bumps

I love argument. I love debate.
PRIME MINISTER MARGARET THATCHER (OCTOBER 13)

Venus bestows kindness, diplomacy, and charm to your Libra girl-friend. She also bequeathed her the lesser traits of vanity and criticism.

Ever had to wait for your Libra to show up for lunch? Or were late to the movies because she wasn't ready when you arrived to pick her up? Being chronically late is one of your Libra pal's most patience-testing traits.

She's so picky about her looks that she can literally try on every-thing in her closet in order to look just right. To her, "just right" means perfect. Perfect for playing golf, the perfect casual outfit for a day of shopping, the perfect jeans and beaded top for a night of dancing. Once that task is finished, she moves to the bath for her beauty ritual, hair, and makeup. She forgets about you, about the time, about everything but looking good.

Why? Because vanity-driven Venus is her ruling planet and Venus refuses to look anything but h-o-t. Take a look at the astrology glyph for Venus: ♀. It's a hand mirror. If it makes you feel any better, your Libra chum doesn't intend to offend. I know that won't matter when you miss the curtain at the play and are stumbling to your seats over the feet of angry patrons who arrived on time. You won't care whether she intends it or not when you're tapping your toes for the zillionth time, sitting on her sofa while she's still in the shower.

How do you break her of this habit? You can't totally. However, you can lessen the affects. Call it to her attention in a nice way. Never say, "You're always late."

I have a Libra friend who was chronically late for everything. No matter how she tried, she consistently forgot the time once she got in front of her mirror. If it's a casual thing like a day of shopping or a lunch date, tell her to call you as she's leaving her house. You have errands to run and don't want to be late to meet her. If you're picking her up, use the same idea. "Call me when you're ready to go." Imply the errands or some work that you have at home to do first. If reser-vations are involved in any way, back the start time up in proportion to the usual amount of time she's late. A half-hour, an hour, and so on.

She's a smart girl and will get your message. She'll try hard to do better, too. It might not work all the time, but it will considerably improve both her timeliness and your mood.

When she's feeling insecure or lacking for attention, she can act shallow and manipulative. She might beat you over the head with how many men are trying to bed her, especially if you are loverless at the moment. She could start a conversation by saying that she doesn't want to hurt your feelings, then go ahead and do just that by criticizing your hair or clothes or current boyfriend.

In both instances, it's usually a temporary slip and doesn't happen often. Her green-eyed Venus jealousy is rearing its ugly head, and it happens when she feels that you are having all the fun or getting more attention. That doesn't change the fact that it either hurts or pisses you off. The ideal thing is to be the better person and ignore her. If you aren't prone to letting things slide, or if it's becoming a habit and she's acting that way in front of your other pals as well, then call her on it, and be straightforward. Tell her you're happy for her love life but you doubt that every man alive is after her. Use the same carefree tone as she does when she's bragging. Tell her that she did hurt your feelings and that you wouldn't do that to her, and be serious. She'll be shocked, wounded, and immediately insist that she didn't realize how you felt. There's debate in the astrological world whether that's quite true, but in any case, it's good to yank her chain back to reality. It will make her think twice next time.

A little tough love goes a long way with a Libra.

Romance Rating

The best way to mend a broken heart
is time and girlfriends.
ACTRESS GWYNETH PALTROW (SEPTEMBER 28)

A Libra girlfriend's love life is a metaphor for her symbolic Scales. On the one hand, she's choosy. She will weigh each strength and fault of the guy she's dating to see how he measures up to her ideal. On the other hand, she's an absolute sucker for a smooth-talking charmer who says all the right things.

Much has been written about her intense sex drive. However, it's not pure physical desire as with sisters Taurus or Aries. A Libra woman wants the whole package, including moonlight and roses. This is what makes her susceptible to the bad boy with a bouquet of flowers and a smooth line; and where she gets her rep of being a bit of a bed hopper.

The Air signs intellectualize love. Gemini makes it a flirty, fun game. Aquarius wants a lover who respects her need for distance. A Libra pal is ruled by Venus, who *is* the goddess of love. Libra is the original girl who is in love with the idea of love. Even if she's had more men than either she or you can remember, straightforward emotional abandonment is not in her nature. She's not a girl who likes her clothes ripped off in the foyer followed by wild sex on the floor the minute he walks in the door. Even if it's a beer and a friendly chat, she needs the idea of romance and some kind of courting ritual before she can abandon herself. That's what her soul thinks of as the correct order of love. She also can fool herself into believing that, because a man goes through the motions, his intentions are honorable.

Setting a mood is a crucial part of your Libra pal's love life. She will go all out with her best china, candles, wine, and spend a couple of hours arranging and rearranging the table, the music selections, and herself before her guy shows up. If they're at a restaurant she'll want to linger over dinner staring into each other's eyes and then slow-dance the evening away while the sexual and sensual tensions build. She knows how to flatter a man's ego and charm him with small talk, and she expects his admiration and adoration in return. She gets it too, for awhile.

After a month, or a year, or ten years of marriage, playing Romeo to her Juliet gets pretty tiring for the average guy, and the relationship can end up as doomed as those star-crossed lovers. It either ends or turns into a passionless sham of smoke and mirrors. Sometimes a Libra woman is so stuck within the illusion of love, intellectualizing what it should be versus emotionally accepting how it changes over time, that she loses it entirely.

Or she realizes she's been had in the worst way when her ideal man with the perfect manners, dress, wit, and charm turns out to be a bastard who practices his line on other women. When this happens, she'll use every one of her wiles to bring him into line, including her skill as a seductress. She's willing to sit up all night talking out their problems. She may cry. She will offer suggestions and options. What she won't do is kick his ass out the door and toss his clothes after him. It's highly unlikely that she'll throw anything at his head either. Libra is the one sign in the zodiac that hates emotional outbursts or confrontations worse than sister Pisces.

Fear of being alone can keep her in a bad relationship long after she's given up. Even if they are sleeping in separate rooms, it's likely that she'll stay until she finds another man or the current one moves out. Similar to sister Gemini, it's easier for Libra to leave when she has another guy lined up.

During the trouble, she'll need to be in constant contact with you. She needs a sounding board. She'll spend hours and hours analyzing and rationalizing their issues. She'll listen to and appreciate your advice. But, it can still take her years to break it off. Even then she might try to remain friends with him on some sort of level. Letting go can be as impossibly hard for a Libra girl as for any Water sign. Your job is to listen, empathize, and keep making suggestions. It's about all you can do. It's a shame, too, because she can waste so much of her life caught in relationship hell.

When you're in the same boat, she will stick by you. You can call her at any hour. She'll do all the things you would expect your best pal to do when you're hurting. She will also have a plan to save you. She won't understand why you don't walk out. She will think you need a doctor if you put up with the slob. How double standard is that? Totally. Her rational, analytical side only works well when it's directed outward. When she's caught in the turmoil she gets forest-for-the-trees syndrome. She refuses to listen to her intuition over her intellect and can end up suffering.

In the man-spotting department, a Libra friend is like Aries and Leo in that she likes all of the attention to be on her, and she's not quite above shoving past you to ask the cute guy at the bar to dance. You can try the I-saw-him-first-rule. Sometimes it works, sometimes it does not. It depends upon which way her Scales are swinging that night.

Bitch Factor

I think I can deceive people.
I'm like the nice, sweet girl when you meet me.
ACTRESS ALICIA SILVERSTONE (OCTOBER 4)

Unbalanced Libras sway from terminally indecisive to manically man-ipulating.

First is hand-wringing, shoulder-shrugging Wishy-washy Juanita, who gets a headache choosing between the fish or chicken. Take her shopping and she'll try on every thing in every store and never make a purchase. Ask her to delegate a project at work and she'll freeze because she can't decide who should get how much of what to do.

Juanita is pathologically unable to make a decision. This is because she really wants everything handled for her. If she had it her way, Juanita would be fed, bathed, dressed, and escorted everywhere.

You have it your way, and tell her you've decided that she should hit the road.

The Vamp is the next swinger on Libra's off-kilter Scale. This vain, self-centered, mirror kisser doesn't want friends. She wants a fan club. As far as Ms. V is concerned, the only reasons other people exist are to fawn over her and fight to sit beside her at dinner.

Her hand-picked inner circle usually consists of girls whom she thinks of as inferior. She thinks she's either cuter, smarter, or that her social skills are better. What she's most capable of is snagging more drunks in the bar. The Vamp is easy to spot because of her rigid back and permanent smirk. If she walks your way giving you the queen's wave, you give her a one-fingered salute and stand aside.

Last and nastiest is Ms. Stage Manager, who uses her considerable Libra charm to manipulate every relationship she can, including yours. She'll flatter her boss into giving her tasks to another coworker while she takes the day off. She'll take your side in a feud, listen to you vent, then run to your enemy and tell her everything. This ploy is designed to get you two at each other's throats while she moves in and takes over the project or promotion.

This bad girl is so phony that she can deliberately pretend that you are her best friend in order to get something from you. Her favorite sport is man stealing. She'll go to any length, even offering advice when you're having a tiff. While she's got one arm around you in false empathy, she's sliding her other well-manicured hand up his sleeve. She'll offer to buy him a drink and to lend a sympathetic ear. If he innocently accepts, Ms. Stage Manager will make sure they go to your favorite hangout and will drape herself over him, hoping one of your friends will see them.

This one is a two-faced pro at twisting the facts. The best way to deal with her is to call her on her bad behavior. Confronting Ms. SM is like throwing a bucket of water on the Wicked Witch of the West. She'll disappear in a hissing cloud of green steam.

Bondability

Sister of the soul: Virgo, Libra, Pisces
Inner circle: Aries, Taurus, Gemini, Aquarius
Party pal: Leo, Scorpio, Sagittarius
Casual chum: Cancer, Capricorn
Famous Libra friendship: Naomi Watts and Nicole Kidman (a Gemini)

♎

Venus in Libra

Venus is at home in Libra and, being in her natural sign, can turn the most aloof Aquarius or reserved Virgo into a hopeless romantic.

Venus Libra cherishes and cultivates close relationships, adds social flair to the most practical Sun, and is in love with love. Your Libra Venus pal is gracious, kindhearted, and usually has a strong interest in the fine arts. Venus here bestows a cultured outlook and desire to be part of the cream of the social crop to the most down-to-earth Sun.

Libra Venus wants to look her best all the time, even when she's exhausted or under the weather. She's a bit of a witch in summoning up a certain look or smile to light up her face and project the image she wants. She can also be so preoccupied with her mirror that she becomes obsessive about every wrinkle. Venus in Libra makes any Sun sign more inclined toward plastic surgery, head-to-toe body-shaping procedures, or anything else that helps her to look young, no matter what her age.

Body adornments of all kinds, including tattoos, appeal to this girl-friend. Depending on her Sun sign, she can opt for anything from an armful of bangle bracelets to full body art.

Libra Venus adds a feminine, romantic touch to any Sun sign's fashion style. The earthiest tomboy will pair a delicately beaded sweater with her jeans, and an ardent fashion rebel is likely to have a few lace-trimmed or ruffled pieces hanging in her closet.

Moon in Libra

No matter how stubborn or hotheaded her Sun sign may be, every Libra Moon girlfriend is something of a diplomat. This Moon makes the most opinionated Aquarius or inflexible Taurus more likely to compromise. Because it also adds Libra's critical and self-indulgent traits to the Sun sign character, it can make a discriminating Virgo even pickier and push a selfish Aries to wild self-indulgence.

A Libra Moon adds an increased sensitivity to other people's reactions to the emotional character. She is more likely to think before she leaps into any close relationship. This girlfriend doesn't fall at first sight for either a new BFF or lover. In fact, she can be a bit calculating to see if you measure up first, either by having the right social connections or being intellectually compatible.

This Moon makes every Sun sign more attuned to, and affected by, her surroundings. She'll most likely take pride in her home and make a painstaking effort to make it a beautiful and tranquil retreat. And while she loves decorating her pad and entertaining friends, she's one of the least domestic creatures in the Universe. This Moon Child is most likely to have a housekeeper, cook, or whole staff of servants, depending upon what her budget will bear.

Unfortunately, this Moon's loyalty can sometimes vacillate, and you might not know exactly where you stand as her friend. It adds a frivolous edge to the emotions. It also makes this girlfriend try to please so many people at once that she ends up making everyone angry!

Your Libra Guy Pal

Your Libra buddy is great for bouncing ideas around. Whether you're considering a career move, an investment, or where to go on vacation, this buddy loves to help you to weigh the pros and cons. If he's not up on the subject, he'll ask around until he finds the right information for you.

He'll also help you in every other way he can. Be sure to reciprocate. He's all about balance, and building a good friendship with him means being available when he needs a favor from you.

When it comes to romance, he's one of the champs. When you need advice, ask him. He can see both sides of a situation and often will point out something that you didn't think about. Not many men will confess much of their real feelings when it comes to love. However, your Libra buddy is more inclined to check your opinion when he has girl trouble than are most of your other guy pals.

He is another social man who is great to call when you want a dance, dinner, or movie partner. He likes getting dressed up and will be as at ease in evening attire as he is in his jeans. His friendly nature makes him popular with everyone from your mom to your boss. He's also a charmer, so expect him to flirt with all your girlfriends.

This cutie is vain, so make sure to compliment him on his shirt or tie, or his choice of restaurants. He's great at small talk and will chat for hours with you over a drink after work. He's another guy who loves a good debate and can argue both points of view, so feel free to choose a side and make your case.

Your Libra buddy is sweet, loyal, and charming. You can't ask for much more.

Chapter Eight
Scorpio

October 23–November 21
Element: Water
Quality: Fixed
Symbol: The Scorpion
Ruler: Pluto
Birthstone: Topaz
Colors: Maroon, burgundy, mahogany
Flowers: Rhododendron, chrysanthemum, honeysuckle
Fragrances: Ylang ylang, vanilla, eucalyptus, and mint

Soul Design

Normal is in the eye of the beholder.
COMEDIENNE WHOOPI GOLDBERG (NOVEMBER 13)

Intense.

Subtle.

Jealous.

Despite the sometimes scary astrological descriptions of Scorpio, this girlfriend is not a control freak who's hell bent on revenge over every real or imagined slight. Neither is she a sexual sorceress trampling over the worn-out bodies of her lovers. She has powerful emotions that she doesn't give lightly, either in love or friendship. Your Scorpio pal keeps her own counsel. So how do you win her friendship? By winning her trust, and that takes time.

Never assume that she operates on the same level as the rest of us. She doesn't. She lives in a protected shell like sister Cancer, but without the overt demands or neediness that the Crab can display. She's *Feminine Fixed Water*. Her Feminine nature is receptive and subtle. Her Water nature means she feels things first, then thinks about them. Being Fixed Water means her emotions rarely change.

Your Scorpio girlfriend is ruled by Pluto, the mythical Lord of the Underworld. He transported the dead across the River Styx and guarded the entrance to the afterlife to ensure that no one escaped. He was constantly on guard and suspicious of everything that moved. Pluto is also associated with destruction (death) and regeneration (rebirth). Pluto is extremely powerful, and the power is that of domination and control.

The old saying, "Still water runs deep," fits the Scorpio girl's character. Winning her trust isn't easy, because she can be as suspicious as Pluto and as emotionally guarded. She's not into superficial emotions and is never anyone's instant new best friend. It takes time for her to commit, but when she does she feels it on a soul level and will do anything to protect and preserve your bond.

Her home base on the zodiac wheel is the Eighth House of Death and Regeneration. Mystical and mysterious, it rules the life forces. Birth, death, sex as a soul connection, the afterlife, psychic power, and spiritual transformation are here. So are things inherited or received from other people, including the family emotional baggage. It's the source of your Scorpio pal's instinct for secrecy. This heavy-duty home is full of plot twists and intrigue—kind of like living with the Sopranos.

Moving here from the sociable, swinging Seventh House of multiple partners and endless cocktail party gossip, the soul becomes reclusive and serious. Unlike the merry Seventh House, where the lights are on and the welcome mat is always out, the Eighth House is shuttered and alarmed. Not many people are allowed entrance.

Remember in the Leo chapter where I suggested treating your Lion pal like your favorite kitty? Your Scorpio girlfriend is more like a wild kitten that you have to approach slowly, building trust a step at a time. You have to be scrupulous in keeping her secrets and respecting her privacy. Her privacy can include where you went for lunch. You might not understand it, but if you want to get close to her, do it.

Don't think she won't find out if you do chat her up to your other chums. She will. A Scorpio pal has an uncanny nose for ferreting out the truth. When her doubt meter is on, it isn't above her to tell you a little tidbit, then sniff around to see whether you've shared it with anyone. Even if it's something as simple as how to contact that great new doctor who's into holistic medicine, or the name of the boutique where she buys her gorgeous shoes, asking her if it's okay to share it with another friend is best. She won't mind. You will move up a notch on her trustworthy meter.

The point is that she needs to be the one to share, even by saying it's okay for you to tell. Sure, it can be irritating. Especially if you are an outgoing Fire or Air sign. Her soul's perspective is that if you tell a little, you'll tell a lot. She has to be in control, and that includes the minutiae of her life. It's her choice what to reveal, not yours, not even to your mutual friends.

Her common astrological symbol is the Scorpion. As scary as it looks, it's not an attack creature. It is tough. Scorpions will fearlessly fight enemies much larger and stronger without hesitation. They will also sting themselves to death if they're cornered before they let any-thing else kill them. However, the Scorpion only uses its stinger for self-defense.

So does your Scorpio pal. Ever argued with a Scorpio? Bring up a burning issue and she'll usually respond quietly. You persist. She lis-tens. She doesn't shower you with rationalizations as the Air signs do or bicker with you as a Fire sign would. Push her and she'll snap back, but she'll rarely raise her voice. In fact, she won't say much at all. This might lead you to believe you've won. Wrong. She's thought about it and decided it's not worth harming your friendship over. Push her too hard, and you'll see the destruction of your friendship. No second chances. Considering it takes almost deliberate thoughtlessness or meanness to bring her to that state, you'll deserve everything you get.

Before Pluto was discovered, Mars was regarded as the ruler of Scorpio and is still considered an influential part of its makeup. I men-tion this because I think it helps to clarify the feeling that something's always going on underneath the surface with your Scorpio pal. Smoldering, like those deep pools of lava that can simmer under the volcano for hundreds of years. When they erupt, there's nothing you or anyone on Earth can do to stop the mayhem. Pluto the Lord of the Underworld, blended with Mars, the God of War. That's Scorpio anger. You may never see a true eruption, but she has the capability of going off like Mt. St. Helens. Just so you know.

I've had lots of Scorpio friends, from casual chums to inner-circle close. Whether she was the outgoing, chattier type that astrol-ogy books refer to as a "sunny" Scorpion or the classic Scorpio who is a quiet observer, these friends had one thing in common. Each of them guarded her privacy like sister Capricorn guards her portfolio. Bombard her with questions about her personal life, and she'll keep the answers chatty and superficial. Start prying and she'll either change the subject or lie. She has no qualms about it if she thinks you are going too far. Probe too soon too fast and she'll simply delete your number from her cell.

As a Water sign, she likes solitude. In fact, she will probably choose to stay home one or two nights a week. She isn't rejuvenating like Pisces or destressing like Cancer. She enjoys her own company and doesn't need others to entertain her. You might know her for years and rarely be invited to her abode. Don't take it personally. Your Scorpio chum's home is her sanctuary.

Astrology has assigned another symbol to your Scorpio pal that illustrates the nature of her spiritual side: the Phoenix. That magical, mythical bird was periodically destroyed, then reborn from its own ashes. No matter how many times it "died," the Phoenix always regenerated. This BFF has incredible willpower. When she wants something she simply never gives up trying. When she has trouble she never gives in, and when she suffers real loss you won't find her wallowing in self-pity. She'll pull herself together and figure out a way to start over and rebuild the portion of her life she lost, whether it's a career change, a divorce, or a serious health issue. This is Scorpio at her best. Your Scorpio friend will help you in the same way.

A close Scorpio girlfriend of mine volunteers for a nonprofit organization. One year, at the absolute last and worst possible minute, a crisis occurred in the organization and everything from the inside out threatened to fall apart. While everyone scrambled to stay on track, they also felt panicked. What the hell had happened and who was to blame? My Scorpio friend simply said, "How can we fix it?" and "How can I help?" It didn't matter to her how it happened or whether anyone was to blame; all she focused on was the solution.

She's complex. She's secretive. You may never quite figure her out. You don't have to. All you need do is to treat her with respect and keep her confidences. It's simple. Take time to win her trust, and you'll discover that beneath the inscrutable demeanor she often shows the world is an extremely sensitive and tenderhearted girl. She takes her friendships as seriously as she does anything else in life, which makes you lucky when she bestows it on you. This girlfriend takes loyalty to a new level. She'll do anything for you, including jumping on the next plane to Brazil to break you out of jail. She could do it, too.

Groove Meter

I'm sure the way to be happy is to live well beyond your means.
ACTRESS RUTH GORDON (OCTOBER 30)

Your Scorpio girlfriend throws herself into everything she does, including play. She's fearless. Want to go bungee jumping or slide across a jungle river on a rope? This is the girlfriend to ask. She'll parasail down a beach or trek to the edge of a volcano with you.

All Water signs are drawn to anything from beach parties to a stroll in the sand. Your Scorpio girlfriend will also like going on a girls-only weekend cruise. Invite her for a day sail around the lake or sheltered harbor on a private boat, then have lunch at the marina so that she can see the ocean. Have connections at the yacht club? This girl will adore sipping a drink and lounging in a plush deck chair while you set off for a day or overnight trip.

If you scuba dive or snorkel, ask her to join you. Discovering what lies beneath the waves appeals to her mysterious side. She'll also join you in the lap pool at the gym, and she'll compete with you to see who can churn out the most turns.

Your Scorpio pal enjoys periods of solitude, as do sisters Cancer, Capricorn, and Pisces, and she might not want to link up every time you ask. When she is ready to have fun, she's up for anything from quiet and elegant to loud and rowdy. She's another girl whose main pleasure is to be with you and her other close friends.

No matter how old she is, a Scorpio woman will enjoy a weekly night out with the girls. It can be anything from getting together to play cards to a progressive dinner to having drinks at the neighborhood pub. Having a standing date with you and her chums makes her feel connected, and she's another sign that is more comfortable partying with her regular crowd.

Invite her to a murder mystery weekend where she can put her natural detective skills to work. Scorpio girls are often interested in the supernatural, so ask her to go with you for a Tarot card or palm reading.

Your Scorpio girlfriend is another pal who makes a great gym buddy. She'll stick with you through the most grueling workout program and won't give up until you both reach your goals. She'll like to go for a bike ride in the park or will run with you on an indoor track.

It's easy to plan a party in her honor. She likes a surprise, and won't care whether the event is casual or formal. Your Scorpio girlfriend's life usually overflows with caring for other people. Her birthday is the perfect time to pamper her.

If your budget allows, or should you decide to buy a group gift, send her to a day spa, or consider buying her a week's worth of home-chef-prepared dinners or a month of housekeeping service. A less expensive idea might be to fill a pretty basket with a pair of luxurious towels and an assortment of spa scrubs, bath oil, lotion, and candles that you've hand-picked in her favorite exotic scents. When buying books, think mystery, romance, and horror novels. Some Scorpio women love vampire romance or serial killer thrillers too.

Her bridal shower can be anything from an informal backyard luncheon to an elegant sit-down dinner, and this is the party to include everyone she knows. A Scorpio chum is somewhat of a traditionalist at heart, so stick to her favorites with the food and keep the decorations simple.

Although she will be gracious about every gift she receives, she has definite tastes. Unless you're close enough to her to know what those are you should pick something from her bridal registry. A Scorpio girlfriend is not flexible about adding a set of modern-designed mugs to her antique teacups, or vice versa.

She'll like satin or silk sheet sets either in traditional eggshell, rich maroon, or black. Consider an electric coffee mill and sample packs of different blends of beans. If she's a tea drinker, choose an electric teapot and include a sampler of rare teas.

Think erotic versus blatant sex with sensual gifts. Tuck a bottle of warming body oil in with a pair of black lace panties or give her a bottle of champagne, two crystal glasses, and a pocket-sized copy of the *Kama Sutra*.

Your Scorpio girlfriend is gutsy, devoted, and will surprise you with her sense of adventure. She's ready to dance the night away one night and board a plane with you to investigate the mystery of the Sphinx the next.

Speed Bumps

I don't have pet peeves. I have whole kennels of irritation.
COMEDIENNE WHOOPI GOLDBERG (NOVEMBER 13)

A Scorpio girlfriend is a bit of a challenge, especially when she keeps trying to take the reins in your relationship. Plus, she doesn't like compromise. Combined, these two traits can turn her into a bit of a control freak.

She doesn't demand to have her way, as a Fire sign would. In fact she can be so nice about changing your lunch date five times in a row that you'll think she's only in an exceptionally disorganized state. When she also decides that she'll only go to a certain bar, or that it's really too far to drive out of her way to a new theater in your neighborhood, you'll begin to get the feeling that you're being had. You are.

One of my Scorpio girlfriends had the worst habit of continually rescheduling her lunch dates. It didn't matter whether it was me, a group of us, or her coworkers, nine times out of ten she would call or email the day before to beg off. Her excuse was that she was always too busy. As patient as I tried to be, after several broken dates, I simply suggested that we postpone indefinitely. She didn't say anything, but she got the message, and the next time she made a date she kept it.

Understand that when she's in control mode, it isn't ego driven or because she thinks you owe her anything. It's her soul's need both to assert its power and test your loyalty. Giving in to her occasional fits of domination is frustrating, but if you can manage to smile awhile, you'll deepen your friendship bond. Making a few concessions will earn you her devotion, because, in her mind, you're proving your loyalty. If she goes overboard, mention it. Don't start a fight, because you never want to get into a battle of wills with a Scorpio.

She's subtle. A Scorpio girlfriend isn't totally selfless in her relationships. She seeks value, like sister Taurus. But where Taurus wants loyalty and security, Scorpio wants loyalty and something from you. She admires power and can be a little opportunistic. If you can help her to get something she wants, she'll stick a bit closer to you than to the rest of the group. Why should she do the legwork if you're willing to help, or do it for her? Once she's gotten what she's after, she might back off a bit. If she's blatantly picking your brains or trying to make you do her thinking for her, give her enough information so that she can track down the rest alone. If it's a report at work or school, send her an Internet link so she can do the research online. Once she's into it, she'll like hunting down the facts, and she'll respect you for not being a pushover at the same time.

She can hang onto her negative feelings. When a Scorpio girlfriend is down, she wants everyone to get down with her. She can refuse to let you even try to cheer her up. But instead of staying home, as a Cancer or Capricorn will, or talking out her troubles as a Gemini or Libra will, she wants to vent to you, long and loudly. You try to listen. You want to help. Soon you get the feeling that your head is stuck in a fan blade with no way out. This is the time when she's feeling the most insecure. The more frightened she is, the meaner she can get. She could snap off a few nasty remarks to you in the middle of her rant. Try to be as patient as you can. Send her a thoughtful card, or leave a small box of chocolates or a whimsical little gift on her desk. You can't always reason with your Scorpio pal when she's this upset. You can reassure her that you are always there for her. If you simply want to slap her instead of toughing it out until her better half reappears, I don't blame you. However, try not to or you'll crush her.

Your Scorpio girlfriend wants to play by her rules. She can be intense, and sometimes her rules are unfair. Yet, she doesn't toss huge boulders in your buddy path. Her friendship is more like a cobblestone road that's consistently a little bumpy with an occasional dip. It's up to you, but traveling it can be a lot more intriguing than zipping down one of those boring turnpikes.

Romance Rating

Women are cursed, and men are the proof.
COMEDIENNE ROSEANNE BARR (NOVEMBER 3)

Your Scorpio girlfriend is deeply loyal, very affectionate, and überdemanding. The black-and-white viewpoint that comes with being a Fixed sign is focused through her possessive Water nature, and when it comes to love, there is absolutely no compromise.

She's never casually involved, even in a short-term affair. She has the most complex emotional structure in the zodiac. There's no halfway. Her love switch is either on or off. She's totally devoted or totally not interested. If he betrays her, she's totally interested in cutting his balls off with a dull blade.

When she's in love, she will offer her man everything, at first. She's a great hostess, his most devoted supporter, faithful and protective. She'll cook dinner, scrub his back in the tub, and give him as much sex as he can survive. She makes herself indispensable to him, but if she isn't careful, her devotion becomes manipulation. In love, as in everything else, a Scorpio girl wants to be in control. She doesn't do this because she's the calculating bitch, as she is sometimes painted. Her only desire is to be part of a close, committed relationship. However, her tendency to be so unreasonably possessive that she can imagine betrayal where none exists can be her downfall.

Her jealously knows no bounds. Suspicion and mistrust are part of her Pluto-ruled soul. If she doesn't consciously act to control her negative side, it blows all out of proportion. She becomes the classic shrew who knows exactly how many minutes it takes for her man to get home from work, and if he's a half-hour late, accuses him of having a quickie with his secretary before leaving the office. Do this over a series of months or years, and she'll lose the lover or husband. He figures if she's going to take him for a bastard, he might as well become one.

When that happens, and he does betray her, it won't matter to her whether she drove him to it or he was a bad boy from the start. She's capable of anything from having her own affair and telling him she did it, trying to make him feel as awful as she does, or tossing his personal belongings out on the lawn and changing the locks while he's at work. After the tirade, she's likely to take him back. But it will never be the same. She may still love him, but a Scorpio girl is nearly incapable of rebuilding trust once it's been broken. Like sister Taurus, she will forgive, as the saying goes, but never forget.

Being the Water sign that she is, this pattern could go on for years. I know a Scorpio girl who's been married to and divorced from the same guy, also a Scorpio, four times. I know of another one who, after divorcing her husband of seven years, proceeded to make it her mission to make his, then his and his new wife's, lives miserable. She used their children together as her pawns. Holidays were canceled, vacations rescheduled, child support renegotiated. She took every opportunity to seek revenge for the next fifteen years. During that time, like the Scorpion who stings itself to death in rage, she never had a decent relationship of her own. She was so hell bent on trying to ruin his life that she ruined her own chances for happiness.

Thank God your average Scorpion isn't quite this intense. However, she can go through several makeup and breakup sessions. When she's hurting she will confide in you. Keep her confidence and don't be judgmental. Let her know that you understand and will stick by her no matter what. That's about all you can do with a Scorpio friend. No one can really help this girl but herself.

When you are in man trouble you couldn't ask for a better friend to stick by you. She will take your side, and if you ask her advice, she will give it to you honestly. She will also keep close check on you by phone and email. She'll help you move, or help you have a garage sale of your ex's power tools should you want a little revenge. She'll tell you that she knew all along he was no good, and she probably did because she's so psychically attuned. Only she didn't mention it because she hoped, for your sake, that she was wrong.

When you're on the prowl with her, you should know that most Scorpio girls are natural man-magnets. This doesn't mean that she's out to win every guy's heart, like Gemini, or deliberately competes with you, like Aries, Leo, or Libra might. On the contrary, when it's girls' night out, she will sit at the table quietly sipping her drink, listening to the conversation, or watching the action. Invariably, the guys will be drawn to her. So, if you aren't the self-confident type, you might have a problem.

Bitch Factor

Until you've lost your reputation,
you'll never realize what a burden it was.
NOVELIST MARGARET MITCHELL (NOVEMBER 8)

Like Macbeth's witches, the only things that Scorpio bad girls are loyal to are themselves and the trouble they like to cause everyone around them.

Least harmful but most obnoxious of this trio is PMS girl. This woman bitches from the time her eyes open until she knocks herself out with a shot and a Xanax at night. Her boss is a jerk. Her boyfriend is a bastard. She's the woman at the office who is forever feuding with one or more of her coworkers. She hates her kids, her dog, and her life.

She's the queen of the small minded, and her only friends belong to that circle of grim-faced gossips who sit around shredding the reputations of everyone they know, including you.

Easy to spot because of her fixed scowl, PMS girl looks at happiness as if it were a disease. The best way to deal with her is to hum your favorite happy tune whenever she's near, and shoot her a big, bold grin the instant she makes eye contact. She'll spin on her cloven hooves and rush off in fear that the sparkle from your friendly smile might strike her blind.

The Control Freak is more subtle and a lot harder to deal with, as she'll move in slowly under the pretense that she likes you. She can appear to be decent, and you might fall for her act, at first. Soon, you'll realize that this pseudo-friendship is all one sided—hers. When the girls go to lunch, the Control Freak must pick the restaurant or she'll find an excuse not to show up. Her resolution to every issue at work is to threaten to quit. Unless her man comes home at the exact time each night, she'll threaten to divorce him.

What this oppressive witch wants is to rule the roost, at home, at work, and within her inner circle. Once you figure it out, stand your ground. The next time she tries to turn your group evening at the theater into her evening at the haunted house, refuse to give in. When she calls later to say that she can't make it, tell her thanks for letting you know. You have another friend who can use the ticket. When she tries to intimidate you with not-so-veiled hints about dropping you as a friend, just say, "Buh-bye," and hang up.

Deceitful Donna has the blackest heart in the Universe. If her aim is to have an affair with your man, she'll start dating his best friend to get close to you both. Donna's different from other zodiac man stealers in that she doesn't want to take your man away from you. She wants to have it all—your guy, her guy, and your friendship. And she's capable of carrying on this charade for decades.

When your job is on the line, Donna will cozy up and pretend that she needs your help on a project. While you're pitching in, she's picking your brain to learn everything she can about your job or any inside information you have about the company, all in the name of coworker camaraderie. Turn your back and she'll climb on it to get to your desk.

Trust your gut with this one. Round up your Gemini, Leo, and Taurus girlfriends to help you smoke her out and kick her to the curb. Oh, and never let your guy out of your sight.

Bondability

Sister of the soul: Libra, Capricorn, Pisces
Inner circle: Cancer, Virgo, Scorpio
Party pal: Aries, Gemini, Aquarius
Casual chum: Taurus, Leo, Sagittarius
Famous Scorpio friendship: Goldie Hawn and Sally Field (also a Scorpio)

♏

Venus in Scorpio

Venus in Scorpio adds a healthy shot of pure animal magnetism to any Sun sign. Here, Venus is possessive, jealous, and demanding. This placement gives an all-or-nothing attitude to any Sun sign when it comes to relationships, friendship included. In love, the Scorpio Venus can be preoccupied with total control and is definitely a sex-oriented woman.

Scorpio Venus wants to bond in a spiritual way and is serious about giving and receiving affection and loyalty. With this Venus, any Sun sign will have an extremely sensitive attitude and can be easily upset, especially if she thinks her friendship isn't reciprocated with the same depth of feeling.

In the emotionally lighthearted Air signs, this placement adds a seductive, sultry edge. The Earth signs become more sensual and controlling, the Fire signs, more primal and powerful, and the Water signs, more mesmerizing and intense.

Her beauty ritual is tied to her powerful sensuality. She can prefer dramatic makeovers and switch from subtle and sweet one day to drama the next. Women with Scorpio in Venus often like false eyelashes, wigs, and Hollywood-style sunglasses because they help to project an aura of mystery. Her cosmetics drawer is usually full of every color eye shadow and lipstick, so that she can change her look to suit her moods.

Her fashion style is understated elegance, underscored with sex. For instance, the skirt on her classic business suit will be slit to the knee. Or her modest looking high-necked little black dress will plunge in a backless V-shape to her waist. And even the most prim and proper Virgo will have a drawer full of scandalously sexy lingerie.

Moon in Scorpio

Astrologically, the Moon is said to be in its *fall* in Scorpio, for this is a very difficult placement. Underneath the breeziest surface character of any Sun sign, this Moon constantly churns the emotions.

It takes a long time to win the trust of a Scorpio Moon chum, even more so than a Scorpio Sun's. The most outgoing Suns will be slower to form a friendship bond, and the already hard-to-know ones can become absolutely inscrutable.

A Scorpio Moon child is born with a built-in set of emotional defense mechanisms that might make you think she's a bit paranoid. She will worry about what people think and can be so sensitive that she will perceive a putdown when none was meant. She can be such a truth teller that she becomes confrontational. This Moon never forgets. Whether it's an offhand remark made years ago, or a silly argument that everyone else forgot five minutes later, your Scorpio Moon pal will have the uncanny ability to dredge it up from memory forever.

She'll have secrets that neither you nor anyone else will ever pry out of her. This Moon can bring hidden sorrows and lots of trouble in relationships. Even the friendliest Sagittarius will have a surprisingly moody trait, and the gossipiest Gemini a secretive, serious side. This Moon also makes every Sun more intuitive, and this girlfriend's hunches can be more reliable than other people's facts.

With a Scorpio Moon the chatty Air signs prefer deeper conversations; the bold Fire signs gain focus and drive to succeed at any cost. It enhances the leadership tendencies of the Earth signs and enhances the creativity and staying power of the Water signs.

Your Scorpio Guy Pal

He'll stand by you through thick and thin, for better or worse, forever. Sounds like more than a friendship, doesn't it? It is. For a Scorpio man, every deep relationship is a soul bond. You can tell him anything. He won't act shocked even if he is, and he won't spill your secrets. He'll help you move in or move out of a relationship. If you need protection while you're packing, this guy's like having the Mafia on your side.

President and Scorpio Theodore Roosevelt said, "Walk softly and carry a big stick." This sums up your Scorpion guy chum's personality. Whether he's funny and outgoing or a quiet loner, he keeps his deep emotions close. This buddy will know everything about you long before you find out even a few juicy facts about him. Do not pry into his life. You won't get anywhere. Bombard him with too many questions and he won't stick around long. If you want to be his friend, you have to be patient. Scorpio is the zodiac's most suspicious sign. He doesn't make deep friendships easily because he doesn't take anything or anyone at face value.

Scorpio guys usually have woman trouble from the time they hit puberty. At first he might think you want something from him. Your best bet in winning his alliance is to be sincere. Never flirt with him. Flirting with a Scorpio guy is like pouring gas on a grease fire. He'll think you want to hit the sheets, which he'll be happy to accommodate. You'll lose him as a pal, though, and that's a shame. His love relationships are messy and usually don't last, but Scorpion friendships are lifelong.

Chapter Nine
Sagittarius

November 22–December 21
Element: Fire
Quality: Mutable
Symbol: The Archer
Ruler: Jupiter
Birthstone: Turquoise
Colors: Purple, indigo blue
Flowers: Dandelion, holly
Fragrances: Amber, patchouli, Oriental florals

Soul Design

I bear no grudges.
I have a mind that retains nothing.
SINGER/ACTRESS BETTE MIDLER (DECEMBER 1)

Energetic.

Optimistic.

Tactless.

I've mentioned that no Fire sign is known for its sensitivity. Well, Ms. Sagittarius can sometimes be the most insensitive but well-meaning lady of the zodiac. Don't misunderstand. As a rule, this girlfriend doesn't have a mean bone in her body. She's neither spiteful nor vengeful. She is kind, affectionate, and never knows a stranger. It's her fondness for shooting verbal arrows without considering the consequences that has earned her the Universe's rep of having terminal hoof-in-mouth disease.

Her astrological home is the Ninth House of Philosophy, Higher Learning, and Religion/Spirituality. Key words here are *long-distance travel, study,* and *spiritual or philosophical beliefs.* One way to explain her natural exuberance and optimistic outlook is that, according to reincarnation, her soul has moved here from the mysterious Eighth House home of secretive, suspicious Scorpio. Eighth House issues are all about trust and control. In Sagittarius the soul splits the chains of distrust and oppression to rush headlong into the world, much like a college student on a spring break free-for-all.

The Ninth House soul has expanded the curiosity of her opposite sign, Gemini, from the superficial to a more in-depth study of a variety of subjects, including you. But, she isn't about to interfere in your life. She assumes that you can think for yourself.

Sagittarius is *Masculine Mutable Fire.* Her Mutable Fire produces a steadier flame than either Leo's intense power of the Sun or Aries' volatile Martian energy. As are all Masculine signs, she's assertive and outspoken. Plus, she is ruled by Jupiter, the supreme and jovial king of the Universe who is rather like Father Christmas. Everything about your Sagittarius chum is a little larger than life. She's so honest that you might cringe from one of her offhand remarks. If you ask her for advice she'll give a completely candid, sometimes totally tactless, answer.

Expansion is the key word for this best friend. She wants to explore life, whether around the neighborhood or around the world. She can be surprisingly philosophical and have an acute sense of a person's inner motivation. She can also talk nonstop for hours about the most ordinary issues.

She's extravagant and sometimes wasteful. This girl can charge the numbers off her credit card to revive her wardrobe or redecorate her home. Unlike Leo and Libra, who'll overspend to get a luxury item, or Capricorn, who would rather have one great piece of art than several cheap ones, your Sagittarius pal thinks more is better and having the most is best.

She also has no qualms about dumping everything a few months later on a whim. She may fall for a new furniture style or decide she doesn't really like that yellow wall. So she cheerfully redoes it all and sells her almost-new things for a fraction of the cost at the local flea market. Jupiter girls know no boundaries.

This includes friendship. As Gemini and Aquarius, a lady Archer has an eclectic group of pals. Whereas Gemini makes casual friends with lots of people and Aquarius keeps her various girlfriend groups separate, Ms. Sagittarius considers them all closer than casual chums and loves the excitement of bringing them all together at one big bash. The bigger the variety in personalities, the better. She's not preachy or prejudiced, and she won't tolerate the bitchiness that can happen in other cliques. If you don't like everyone she likes, she doesn't care, but you had better get along with everyone when she's around. She won't hesitate to call anyone on their bad behavior, any place, any time.

A freedom-loving Sagittarius BFF needs plenty of space. How then do you get her to spend more time with you? Be flexible. Her Mutable Fire is more action oriented than Aries. Let her know that you are always ready to shop, have lunch, get a mani/pedi, or head for a movie after work, and you'll stay high on her friends-to-call-first list. Be available for her, too. She's forever helping others, so the simple act of remembering to ask her if she's okay or if she needs something will rack up lots of pal bonus points.

She's openhearted. A Sagittarius girlfriend of mine remembers everyone's birthdays, the names and birth dates of their men, kids, and pets, and is always doing someone a favor. She sends cards for every holiday and is always ready to help even in a minor crisis. Her parties are a legend in our group. Jupitarian feasts of food and drink to be celebrated with a group of her 100 closest friends. Only when she says that, she means it. She knows everyone intimately, from their health issues, to family feuds, to work problems, to who's falling in love and who's contemplating divorce. She's a people magnet because she genuinely cares about our lives.

So does your Archer chum. Want to paint your bedroom? She'll shop with you for the right color, then show up with a couple of extra friends to help get the job done fast. That way you'll have more time to party afterward. She'll drive her car for a girls-only getaway and make the trip arrangements. Yes, many signs are generous. The fabulous thing about a Sagittarius pal is that her friendship comes with no strings attached. She doesn't need reciprocation. She will absolutely be thrilled if you bring her a thank-you gift. However, her soul operates from Jupiter's benevolence, and she offers to help because it makes her feel good, not because she expects something in return.

She also has Jupiter's wrath. All Fire signs have to blow now and then. It clears the air and is exhilarating—for them. Aries does it to get attention. Leo does it because you're not paying attention. Sagittarius does it out of a perceived disrespect. Jupiter was boss god. If he wanted to play the clown, he would. Try to make him look like a clown, or take advantage of his goodwill, and you got it right in the head with a bolt of lightning.

Sagittarian anger usually erupts like a spout of dragon flame, scorches the ears off anyone within hearing distance, then subsides as quickly and is forgotten—by her. She's capable of shooting caustic verbal arrows and yelling at the top of her lungs one minute and being her normal, happy self the next. The good thing is that this girlfriend rarely holds a grudge. She doesn't have the heart or the time for it. Plus, it takes a lot to provoke her real anger. Consider yourself warned.

She's not vain. Yes, she's sexy. Yes, she likes to look her best. Yet, you won't see her preening like Libra or Leo. She doesn't necessarily follow every fashion trend as Gemini, and unlike Capricorn, designer knockoffs will suit her fine. This chum will have a closet of comfortable clothes and isn't into changing her looks every season. If she has short hair at twenty, chances are it will still be short at sixty.

Your Sagittarius pal isn't afraid to try anything once or to make a fool of herself in the process. One of her best qualities is her ability to laugh at herself. Of course, this means that she'll laugh as loud and long at you should the occasion arise. You might be temporarily embarrassed, but unless you're totally thin skinned, you can't stay mad at this good-natured girl.

Her astrological symbol is the mythical Centaur. Armed with a bow and arrow, this half-human, half-horse creature, although compassionate and wise, could never be tamed. The Centaur understood the "beastie" side of humankind as well as the spiritual one. Your pal understands that each of us has a dark side. It's one reason she accepts people warts and all. No one is perfect. She doesn't try to be. She doesn't expect you to be. How refreshing is that?

She's a little over the top, and her life is an open book. She can be rowdy. She can spend money as if she had a printing press in the basement. But, if you're looking for a devoted, perpetually optimistic BFF who isn't high maintenance, you couldn't find anyone more perfect.

Groove Meter

*When people keep telling you that
you can't do a thing, you kind of like to try it.*
FORMER SENATOR MARGARET CHASE SMITH (DECEMBER 14)

The first rule to remember about your Sagittarius chum's party style is that there are no rules. This girlfriend is up for anything, any time, anywhere. *Live in the moment* is her maxim. She's so spontaneous that she can make a flitting Gemini look dull.

Most Sagittarius girlfriends are interested in far-off places. If you're the adventurous type you'll skip ahead to the front of her friendship line. A Leo pal will head to the nearest theme park with you. Your Sagittarius buddy will do that too. She'll also fly with you to Africa or help you to navigate the Amazon. Instead of talking about the Great Wall of China or life in a Tibetan monastery, she would love to see for herself. She was born with a yen to travel, and if time and money allow, she'll accompany you to anywhere in the world.

Sagittarius girlfriends are born knowing how to get the most out of life. Want to have a weeklong shop-a-thon at every megamall in your state? Call her. She won't care whether you're cruising around town or on a day trip to a cultural exhibit, all that matters is that she stays on the move.

Lots of Archers like to gamble, so take her to a casino or to church on bingo night. She'll like the horse races because it's outdoors, full of excitement, and she can scream and jump up and down. She usually likes sports, but prefers to play rather than sit on the sidelines.

A Sagittarius chum loves to throw parties. In addition to the usual birthdays and anniversaries, this girlfriend will have theme parties for big events such as Super Bowl Sunday or the Kentucky Derby, complete with coordinating decorations. She'll also toss an Academy Award night bash and ask everyone to dress formally.

Her sense of adventure extends to food, so don't be afraid to take her someplace new. Spicy foods usually appeal to her, so think Indian, Southwestern, or Asian fusion. She'll sample anything once. Clubbing always appeals to her more-the-merrier soul. This girl thrives in crowds where the dance floor is packed and you have elbow your way to the bar. Ending the evening with a school-style slumber party at either her place or yours is something she likes to do. Then she'll get up and cook breakfast for everyone . . . and start the party again.

As for throwing a bash in her honor, good luck trying to surprise this girlfriend. Before you can make arrangements, she'll send you an invitation to the party she's tossing for herself.

Regarding gifts, she's probably the most easy-to-please woman in the zodiac. She'll be happier that you remembered her than she'll care about what she gets. Think anything from silly to sentimental. She likes to write personal notes, so get her stationery or a box of pretty note cards and a nice pen. If it's books or movies, make it the latest action-adventure or blockbuster. Lessons for the latest Latin dance craze are a good choice. An overnight bag, stocked with trial-sized shampoo, toothpaste, and woodsy-scented soaps and lotions appeals to her ready-to-go nature. If she has pets, and most Sagittarius girlfriends do, including a bag of kitty toys or a chewbone for her dog will please her.

The same goes for her wedding gifts. She is a born hostess and will like gifts for entertaining. Try an ice bucket filled with martini glasses, cocktail napkins, a jar of olives or onions, and plastic picks; or one that is wine themed, with assorted cheeses and fruit. Include a gift card to her favorite beverage store. A popcorn popper is good. So is a shaved ice machine or an electric ice cube dispenser for the patio if your budget allows.

Sex-oriented gifts such as edible undies, chocolate body paint, or a naughty board game will appeal to her rowdy side. Ditto for lingerie. Classic pieces such as a feminine-but-cozy nightgown or brightly colored matching bra and panty sets are good choices. However, she'll also adore barely there thongs, a lace-up bustier, or pair of thigh-high stockings.

Your Sagittarius BFF can dance all night, go home and change clothes, then head out for more fun in the morning. Her energy levels don't decrease much with age, although she may give up running the bases in favor of learning golf.

Speed Bumps

If it's a good idea . . . go ahead and do it.
It's much easier to apologize than to ask permission.
REAR ADMIRAL, U.S. NAVY, GRACE MURRAY HOPPER (DECEMBER 9)

She's so exuberant and on the go that it can be exceptionally hard to pin her down. Your Archer girlfriend's calendar is always packed with social events, errands, and personal appointments. You can start to feel neglected when you can't snag her attention for a lunch date.

Try not to take it personally, because she isn't snubbing you. This might be hard if you're a possessive Earth girl or sensitive Water baby; however, try to understand that her Ninth House soul is on a quest to experience as much as it can on this go-around in life. Remember, the key is to be as flexible as you can. This doesn't mean waiting around for her call, or dumping your other pals should she have a change of plans, but even if you're a routine-loving Taurus or schedule-addicted Virgo, try to make room for a spontaneous outing or two with your Sagittarius chum. She'll also try to juggle her calendar for you.

There's nothing shy about an Archer pal. Neither is she humble, modest, or quiet. You can hear her laugh above a noisy crowd, and she tends to monopolize every conversation by talking faster and louder than anyone else. This Jupiter girl can blurt out as many embarrassing facts about your private life as sister Gemini will. The difference is that Sagittarius can do it in front of the boss or your mom without stopping to think. If she's embarrassing you in public, there's only one thing to do. Walk away. When she's in rambunctious mode, nothing short of a cop can stop her.

Call her on it later and she'll respond with a puzzled look. It was all in fun. Why are you being such a prude? The best thing is to be as plain and outspoken as she would. Tell her straight that her behavior was inappropriate and please don't do it again. If you expect to be friends with her forever, you'll have to repeat this a few hundreds times until she remembers. That's usually after she turns forty.

As with every Fire sign, she'll like to run the show if she can. Aries will gather all the information for a trip, then be hurt if you don't follow her suggestions. Leo will expect to lead the group into the restaurant or nightclub. Your Sagittarius pal will gather the information, set the date, and make the reservations, all on the assumption that when you said you'd like to go to Kenya on safari someday that it meant as soon as possible. This exasperating trait is also endearing, because she'll go out of her way to do all the footwork and planning so that all you have to do is check your baggage and board the plane.

She does the same thing at work, or when you're sharing a project, or she's helping you to plan a party. When you ask her to help, she takes the ball and runs. Jupiter energy knows no bounds and thinks it knows best. She's not being pushy in a malicious way; she's acting on her soul's pattern of benevolent kindness. No matter how she screws it up or misinterprets or leaps before she looks at your expense, her intention is to be helpful.

How do you handle this when all you want to do is scream at her to butt out? Avoid the situation in the first place. If it's a project, give her written instructions on what to do and how you want it done and check in frequently. If it's the trip to Kenya, emphasize *someday* and make it a few years down the road. About ten is good. Anything closer and she's likely to start checking for online deals.

She makes promises that she can't keep. Every Sagittarius girl-friend's nature includes a deep desire to be all things to all people. She'll promise to go shopping with you on Tuesday or meet you for dinner Friday or help you to paint your apartment on Saturday. Trouble is, she's also made similar promises to several of her other friends. She has no choice but to flake out on a few of you. Contrary to her opposite sister, Gemini, whose flaky actions are a result of deciding she's found something better to do, your Sagittarius chum simply overextends herself. She makes promises like she does most things, on the spur of the moment, without checking her calendar, because she wants to be there to help or have fun with you. You can help her to manage her time better by making sure that she does check her calendar before committing herself.

Your Sagittarius best friend does everything with flair, including irking the heck out of you with her sometimes careless behavior. Protect your sanity by helping her to think before she leaps. It won't flatten all of the speed bumps, but there will be fewer in your friendship road.

Romance Rating

Energy is more attractive than beauty in a man.
AUTHOR LOUISA MAY ALCOTT (NOVEMBER 29)

A Sagittarius friend is one of the most hard-to-catch girls in the universe. She can leave a trail of broken hearts from high school to retirement. Even when she is caught, her first marriage is more like a test drive and usually ends in divorce.

Men are attracted to an Archer woman because she is so free spirited, outspoken, and always ready to party. These are also largely the reasons for her long record of dating disasters. She absolutely refuses to be fenced in either by a jealous boyfriend's demand that she stop seeing her platonic guy pals or by her husband's silly assumption that, once married, she'd turn into Helen Homemaker.

All Fire signs require a measure of independence, and the Air signs need some sort of social life. Sagittarius demands her freedom. End of conversation. If she's hooked up with a home-loving Earth or Water guy, she'll probably find a career that allows her to travel three weeks of the month. If she can't do that, she'll become the hostess with the mostest and throw a party on every major and minor holiday. She'll have hellacious screaming matches with her jealous Fire or Air sign lovers that end with her (not him) slamming out the door to meet her friends for drinks. No matter how he tries to pin her down, she'll be two jumps ahead in finding any excuse not to be domesticated. It's not hard to see why your Archer pal can have the longest string of exes under the Sun.

This girlfriend doesn't want a joined-at-the-hip, matching T-shirt type relationship. She needs excitement. Sometimes, she'll find it with someone else, as does sister Pisces. Unlike Pisces, who's after the non-existent ideal love, the Archer seeks the thrill of that new rush of lust and romance.

Even if she's a stay-at-home mom, she'll be the one who's actively involved in the PTA, will have a hobby, or do volunteer work while the kids are at school. She'll also be the one who has Brownie meetings, Neighborhood Watch meetings, and monthly card games at her home. She might decide to sell cosmetics or kitchenware or decorating items through one of those home-based party plan companies. What she won't do is spend all day cleaning and polishing the woodwork.

When the inevitable breakups happen, she'll be as hurt as we all are; however, she'll usually bounce back in a shorter time. Her basic soul design is one of optimism, and she knows that something better is just around the corner. The best way to get her to smile again is to get her out of the house. She's not the type to sit home and sob into her bowl of ice cream. This girl wants to shake off the negative and get back on the positive side of life as quickly as possible.

She will talk about what went wrong. She can get repetitive when something bad happens. Keep listening. It might take her weeks or a couple of months before she quits reliving it, because she can have a hard time understanding what went wrong. All she wanted was for the fun to continue and the romance and to keep in touch with her friends. What she got was a guy who tried to change all the things that made him fall in love with her in the first place. She feels cheated and betrayed. She had to kick him out. Yes, she did. It's his loss, because as much freedom as she demands for herself, this girl is willing to give to her man.

When you're in the same position, your Sagittarius girlfriend will drop everything to be with you. She'll hold your hand, bring you food, even do the dishes and make your bed. She closes the space up tight and stays close until you feel like a human again. She doesn't coddle, and she won't listen to a pity party too long. This girlfriend knows the difference between being there in a crisis and enabling you to wallow in depression. She'll give you what she thinks is enough time to at least quit bawling and put your makeup on again, then tell you it's time to get on with your life. She'll back it up by dragging you out of the house. It doesn't matter where. What matters is that she's right, and you'll feel much better for going.

If you're man scouting together, she'll respect the I-saw-him-first rule. She's neither jealous nor envious. She's so bubbly and outgoing that she attracts her own fan club. In case you feel a little green-eyed toward her, try not to show it because you'll hurt her feelings.

Bitch Factor

I do not want people to be agreeable.
It saves me the trouble of liking them.
AUTHOR JANE AUSTIN (DECEMBER 16)

An Archer's assets of exuberance, honesty, and a flair for entertaining can get expanded into a nightmare of Orwellian proportions.

First and most eternally tiring on the Sagittarius Top Three Bimbos list is Broken Record Barb. She takes the Archer's ability to dominate the conversation and expands it into an all-night nonstop mouth marathon. You could pee your pants waiting for her to take a breath so that you can excuse yourself to go to the powder room.

Worse than Virgo's Trivia Queen, Barb doesn't confine herself to current details. She has to relive everything that's ever happened to her since the black day that she was born. What seems like a harmless conversation invariably turns into a trip down memory lane, with several side trips to pity-party alley. After a few of her filibusters you'll start to act like one of Pavlov's dogs, only you'll be cringing the second you hear her voice on the phone.

Broken Record Barb will never change. She's caught in the myth that her life is the only one that's interesting. You can't shut her up. Save yourself and don't answer the phone. She really won't notice because, being the egotistical bimbo that she is, yours was just the next number on her speed-dial list.

Next is Ms. Name Dropper. This one makes friends for two reasons. You're either someone she's impressed by, or she assigns you slob status and tries to awe you by acting as if she's a part of the in-crowd.

If she attended a political event with 500 other folks, she'll tell you she had lunch with the mayor and that the mayor thought her ideas on reducing pollution were fabulous and wants to hear more. The truth is that Ms. Name Dropper backed the mayor into a corner and bombarded the poor woman with a nonstop barrage of nonsense until the mayor told her to write her a letter just to escape.

She will also pretend to know more than you about any subject under the Sun and try to get you to believe that you can get nowhere without her connections. This offer is always backed up with a negative critique of your project or idea. She would be happy to introduce you to the mayor, but your recycling suggestion won't fly. She knows all. Don't believe her for a minute. If your idea is good, she'll steal it to use to wiggle her way into the power player circle.

You'll know if it's good. If it weren't, this one wouldn't give you the time of day. Let that be your mantra if she comes bounding by.

Reduce the Archer's interest in people to its lowest form and you get Tactless Terry, who barrels through life pretending that her rude and insensitive observations are only her "honest" opinions. In her, that thoughtless but innocent trait turns malicious.

Terry knows that blurting out a painful or embarrassing fact at the worst moment will hurt you. She does it on purpose. Terry takes Gemini's love of dishing rumors about people and expands it into a full frontal assault of brutalizing truth, in the presence of her victim.

Her comments are dispensed in two ways. She's only joking (it's all in good fun and no one will care so you shouldn't either), or she's reluctant (this is for your own good). In the latter, she tries to get you to confess something, because it not only humiliates you, it might inspire someone else within hearing distance to confess a dark secret too. This is her most dangerous ploy, as it only serves to give her ammunition to use against your other friends.

If she knows too much about you, don't get into a word war. Terry won't care if you spill a couple of her darker secrets as long as she brings you down. The best way to handle her is to never tell her anything you don't eventually want thrown back in your face. That way, when you do witness her nasty behavior, you can safely tell her to shut the hell up and get permanently lost.

Bondability

Sister of the soul: Aries, Libra, Aquarius
Inner circle: Gemini, Scorpio, Pisces
Party pal: Taurus, Leo, Virgo, Sagittarius
Casual chum: Capricorn, Cancer
Famous Sagittarius friendship: Katie Holmes and Victoria Beckham
(an Aries)

Venus in Sagittarius

In Sagittarius, Venus never knows a stranger. Cheerful, always in motion, and friendly with everyone, including her in-laws, this girl easily gives her friendship and love.

Everything is an adventure to the Sagittarius Venus, and even the most reclusive Scorpio or reserved Capricorn will have a more carefree attitude about her relationships. Taurus Suns with this placement will be less inclined toward routine, while Gemini Suns can be as hard to pin down as a bee flitting through a garden. Every Sun sign with Sagittarius in Venus will approach life as a journey and need to feel they and their relationships are continually growing and evolving. They see no point in the status quo, and often, this placement will give the most home-loving Cancer a huge case of wanderlust.

This girlfriend may have two jobs, or work in the travel or sports industries or with animals, horses in particular. Whatever she does, she has high standards and pushes hard to succeed.

This Venus's beauty ritual has to be simple and quick, as she travels light and doesn't want to haul an extra bag full of lotions and potions. Cleansers that have a clean, citrus, or woodsy smell; soft, natural eye, lip, and cheek colors; and a light dusting of powder satisfies her. Her hairstyle will be easy to care for; either wash-and-wear short, or long enough to pull into a ponytail.

Her fashion style is just as carefree. Sagittarius Venus prefers comfortable, flowing clothing that won't restrict her movement. You'll find bright colors and easy-care, wrinkle-proof fabrics that pack well in the closet of the most discriminating Capricorn or glamour-loving Leo.

Moon in Sagittarius

Adaptable, sparkling, and open minded are some astrological descriptions of the Sagittarius Moon. Here, the emotional character is optimistic. No matter what happens, this Moon child knows that sooner or later, everything will be okay.

A Sagittarius Moon is bold and independent and can give the quietest Sun a reckless, restless emotional makeup. She's competitive. She's forever comparing herself to everyone around her, including you. This can turn a laid-back Pisces into a workaholic, or make a goal-achieving Capricorn absolutely driven to succeed. However, this Moon is as fair a competitor as she is fierce.

This Moon is charming and funny, and adds a witty edge to the driest Sun sign personality. A Sagittarius Moon child usually looks at life from a perpetually skewed angle and rarely acts moody because she hates emotional scenes. This Moon's natural proclivity is to hold all her angst inside until she explodes. When she does, it's fast and furious, then over as quickly as it started.

The Sagittarius Moon is full of adventure and loves life. These girl-friends want to get the most out of every experience. Fire signs are even more self-confident and less likely to take advice. Air signs can talk you into just about anything. Water signs become much more energetic and philosophical, and the Earth signs are more creative and self-starting.

Your Sagittarius Guy Pal

If you're after a pure play pal who's always ready to party, here's your guy. A Sagittarius buddy is up for anything at any time. He's easy to get to know, and you'll usually find him in the middle of a group of friends laughing about something.

He's honest to a fault, but not the most sensitive guy around. If you ask his opinion, make sure that you can handle the unvarnished truth. This is a buddy whose first inclination will be to get you into bed. He can be a truly irksome boyfriend because he usually doesn't settle down until he's in his thirties. Having him for a buddy is fabulous because this guy was born to have fun.

He loves the outdoors. If you are into anything from hiking, to canoeing, to fishing, ask him along. He'll eat anything. Feel free to invite him for sushi, or Tex-Mex, or a hot dog. He loves sports, so you can include him in your Saturday morning tennis doubles or a Super Bowl party with your other pals.

As talkative as Gemini, your Sagittarius pal has a more philosophical outlook on life. He has big dreams and will be the first one to believe in and support yours. He loves to give advice, so you can ask him anything, as long as it's not about romance. He has a hard time getting a grip on his own feelings, and he's not the best at understanding anyone else's.

He's another buddy who loves his freedom. Don't put too many demands on his time. He doesn't mind helping you move or playing handyman in a pinch, but expect him to constantly come to your rescue and he'll start feeling trapped. That aside, everybody loves this guy. They can't help it. He's open, and funny, and doesn't have a mean bone in his body. Party on!

Chapter Ten
Capricorn

December 22–January 19
Element: Earth
Quality: Cardinal
Symbol: The Mountain Goat
Ruler: Saturn
Birthstone: Garnet
Colors: Deep greens and browns
Flowers: Carnation, poinsettia, gladiola
Fragrances: Grapefruit, jasmine, pine, sandalwood

Soul Design

From birth to age 18, a girl needs good parents,
from 18 to 35, she needs good looks,
from 35 to 55, she needs a good personality,
and from 55 on she needs cash.
AMERICAN ENTERTAINER SOPHIE TUCKER (JANUARY 13)

Patient.

Melancholy.

Opportunistic.

Traditional astrology descriptions of your Capricorn BFF as a thrifty, determined, fashionably chic woman are correct—as far as they go. They make her sound single minded, emotionally cold, and awfully boring, which she is definitely not. A Capricorn pal is fun loving, social, and as full of fun as any girl in the Universe. What sets her apart is that she likes purpose and quality in her life. She wants these traits in her friends, too.

Your Capricorn girlfriend is *Feminine Cardinal Earth*. Her Feminine side is receptive. Her Earth side is practical and values stability. Her Cardinal nature makes her more prone to taking action than sister Taurus, and less likely to discuss the options before she does, as sister Virgo would do. Like sister Virgo, Capricorn is ruled by Saturn. In Virgo, Saturn's energy is lightened up (or watered down, depending on your point of view) by curious, versatile Mercury. In your Capricorn friend, however, Saturn's serious energy is pure and undiluted.

Saturn's message is simple: You get what you work for. Make a goal, be diligent about achieving it, and be sensible. What's a goal without the education to reach it? This doesn't mean a PhD. It means study, focus, and practice. Your Capricorn girlfriend doesn't believe in instant success. She knows the value of time and that it's not limitless. That's why Capricorn is often referred to as the sign of reverse aging. As a child, your Capricorn chum might have seemed mature for her age. She was probably a serious student since grade school, or assumed some family responsibilities at a much earlier age than most kids.

Her soul lives in the Tenth House of Career and Public Recognition. Things associated with the Tenth House are professional success, standing in the community, and achievements and honors. It deals with responsibility. The Tenth House soul has to earn its place in the Sun.

Having moved here from the philosophical, no-boundaries, Ninth House, where socializing is an art form, the soul leaves the party life and gets serious about making a real achievement. It doesn't matter whether it's at a skilled trade or a degreed profession. What matters is that it's the best at what it does.

Her symbol, the Goat, is that sure-footed creature that nimbly jumps over obstacles on its steady progression up the face of the most rugged landscape. Leo's Lion may be King of the Jungle, but Capricorn's Goat is King of the Mountain.

Wanting to be queen of her mountain can turn your Cappy girlfriend into a workaholic in her twenties. While you and the rest of her chums are having fun, she's burning the midnight oil. She can seem so tight with a buck that you think she squeaks when she walks. However, around her mid-thirties, you'll notice that she's starting to play more. And, by the time the rest of you are getting a head of steam up in your careers, she'll be on top of the heap. Of all the girlfriends in the zodiac, this one has the capacity to retire very well off, well under sixty.

A danger for her is burning out at an early age from trying too hard to achieve too much in too short a time. This is the girlfriend who has spent every moment striving to be the top student, the top athlete, the girl with the most extracurricular activities, and on and on until she simply stops one day. Don't confuse it with competitive Aries and her desire to be first. Aries loves to play and does it frequently. Your Capricorn pal isn't the most outgoing of the signs and, as an Earth sign, is very content to stay home. When she's overloaded, she might decide to stay in bed for a week.

When this happens, help her take her mind off herself with some one-on-one time. Go to the park, or spend a day in the mountains. She doesn't need to be entertained. She needs to clear her head, and being outdoors helps her to relax. You can share a picnic lunch or sit quietly listening to the radio or reading your favorite novels. She'll also feel better if on the way home you stop at a good restaurant for dinner. Think quality food, not necessarily the most expensive place in town.

She has a social consciousness. It's likely that she'll be involved in some sort of political activities. Whether it's actively campaigning for her candidate or working on a committee to save a local historical building, a Capricorn chum likes to be involved. She'll attend city council meetings, or work on behalf of a fund-raiser to help the zoo, hospital, or some other local charitable organization. Part of this is her Tenth House soul's need to be in the public eye. Part is her Cardinal Earth's need to be in control of her environment as much as possible.

Her reputation for being luxury loving is true. However, this girl isn't about to blow her budget, as sister Libra can, just to impress the company. Your Capricorn friend would rather have one designer hand-bag that she carries every day than a dozen trendy knockoffs that she can rotate with her outfits. She wants the best, and she'll save her money to get it. She's also a great negotiator and isn't afraid to bar-gain hard to get the most for her money. If you can manage to steer her toward the best of both worlds, designer and sale, you'll climb up a few rungs on her friendship ladder.

Her reserved side isn't due to shyness, as sister Taurus or Virgo can be. She has a more suspicious nature. She doesn't believe in get-ting something for nothing. Rush to become her new best friend, and she'll wonder about your motives. She's also not into playing faithful sidekick. Try to make her a follower in your fan club and she won't waste her time on you. This pal doesn't believe in giving something for nothing. That's why it might take you a little longer to get close to her. Once you do, you'll have a supportive girlfriend who will never hesitate to help.

Integrity is important to your Capricorn chum. It goes much deeper than flaking out or being honest with her. This girl observes how you treat others as well. Not just mutual chums, but your coworkers, your family, and the guy who runs the hot dog stand. If you aren't reliable in your interactions with others, she'll suspect that sooner or later you'll fail her as a friend too. She is understanding; however, she can't tolerate flakiness or mistreatment for too long. This girlfriend doesn't have many I-forgive-you cards in her deck.

She's levelheaded. You can rely on her to give you sensible advice about achieving your own goals. Whether it's keeping you on track with your diet, coaching you for a test, or pitching in to polish your résumé, you can count on her to do her best to help you to succeed. She takes her responsibilities as your friend as seriously as she does everything else. That's why it's important that you always be there for her as well. She is very aware of reciprocation in her relationships. It's not about tit-for-tat payback. It's her integrity rule.

Another trait assigned to her by simple astrology is that she's melancholy, which gives the impression that she's a humorless drudge who lives under a cloud of doom. Next time you read or hear that, think of these women: Diane Keaton, Mary Tyler Moore, Dolly Parton, and Paula Poundstone. Each is a tribute to the carefree and funny side of Capricorn. Her sense of humor is more wry observations about life or a dry wit that pops out so unexpectedly that you're caught off guard.

As Cardinal Earth, her focus on initiating action is in a practical way. Of the other Cardinal signs, Aries bosses, Cancer and Libra are prone to manipulation to get their way—Cancer by emotion, Libra by rationalization. A Capricorn friend simply steps in and takes over.

One of my Capricorn friends is the first person on the phone or at the door should any type of crisis occur at her office, with her family, or among her friends. She literally drops what she's doing and makes sure that everyone's needs are attended to, whether that means cooking dinner for a family in distress or helping a coworker organize a timeline for an important project. She never waits to be asked when she sees that someone needs her help. Yours won't either.

She's earthy, devoted, and fun to be around. A Capricorn girlfriend will support your dreams and help you to lay out a plan for achieving them, then cheer you every step of the way. How classy is that?

Groove Meter

Don't compromise yourself. You're all you've got.
'60s ROCK STAR JANIS JOPLIN (DECEMBER 19)

Your Cappy girlfriend isn't the most sociable creature on the planet. What about all of those glittering opening nights, or gala fund-raisers where you've see her on the arm of a cute guy and networking like crazy? Well, those events serve a purpose. She's being seen. She's making key connections that might help her in either her career or her personal life. How mercenary. Not in the least bit. Her Saturn-ruled soul requires justification for the cost of her gown, trip to the spa, and the hair salon. The outlay has to produce some return.

When she's truly relaxing, her preference is for one-on-one or small group activities. Both Saturn and her Goat symbol are the loners of the zodiac. When practical Saturn plays, he plays with a purpose, and when he rests, he prefers to rest alone. The Goat is not an altogether social animal. While two or three might forage together for grass to munch, you're as likely to see them scattered on the mountain, still within sight of each other, but each happily doing her own thing.

Your Cappy friend does the same thing. If she turns down a girls' night out, don't worry. She's not a party animal and doesn't usually feel the need to go anywhere just to get out of the house, and she rarely bends to peer pressure. This woman enjoys her own company. She doesn't get as bored or lonely as an Air or Fire sign chum can. Plus, she's usually a borderline workaholic who enjoys her quiet time at home, either reading or working on one of her hobbies.

Many Capricorn pals are interested in pottery, ceramics, or woodworking. Invite her to take a Saturday class with you. A one-day intensive lesson might fit best into her busy schedule.

Want to redo your wardrobe? She's your girl. She has an eye for fashion and will be honest, but not brutal, about what looks best on you. The added bonus is that she will respect your budget and tramp all over town with you to find the biggest bang for your buck. Even if she can't afford it, she will love browsing through a designer shoe or clothing store. She's energized by the smell, feel, and look of beautifully made, one-of-a-kind fashions. She'll also sign up for their mailing lists and start saving her money for the sale events.

Invite her to dinner at your place. Whether it's potluck or take-out won't matter. She's another girlfriend who doesn't need anything but to be with her closest pals. She also likes to entertain at home, so you can expect a return invitation.

This is another girlfriend who usually will love to go antique shopping. In addition to snagging something for her décor or a piece of exquisitely handcrafted jewelry, she'll like the tranquility of walking through the store, taking time to look at everything.

In her own, quiet way, your Capricorn BFF is as competitive as sister Aries and hates to lose as badly as does the Ram. Ask her to join your softball team or to be your tennis partner. She's a great team player who will play as hard as she can to win.

She's another sign that loves outrageous humor, so invite her to a comedy club or to catch the latest frat house-style funny movie.

If you're planning a party for her, she'll like to be surprised, provided that you don't suddenly show up on her doorstep, entourage in tow. Take her to dinner or plan something at either your or a friend's place.

A Cappy friend likes quality. Instead of buying her three pairs of inexpensive earrings, select one semi-expensive pair in a classic style that she can wear for years. If it's perfume, make it a more traditional scent or one of the classic fragrances versus one of the latest trendy blends that come and go on the market. With her earthy sense of humor, she'll enjoy a humorous book or a DVD of her favorite silly movie. Scatter a few gag gifts among her present, too. Think fun and value when choosing her gifts.

If her party includes dinner, this girlfriend will enjoy a more formal, sit-down dinner. Choose the best restaurant that you can afford. It doesn't have to be five-star. It does have to serve quality food, with some gourmet touches if possible. Include a bottle of vintage wine, either with her meal or as a gift.

Treat her bridal shower the same way. Choose something simple yet elegant, such as a tearoom luncheon with finger sandwiches served on antique chinaware. Or, a buffet of her favorite home-cooked foods at your house, with each dish cooked by one of her other friends.

Choose gifts either from her bridal registry or to complement her taste and style. She won't know what to do with an odd piece of artwork or offbeat vase, and it will usually end up in her recycled-gift box. Nothing ostentatious, please. Your Capricorn chum isn't impressed by how much it costs. She's impressed by whether the cost matches the value. If she is into antiques, add to her collection, or try to find something that coordinates. She'll also enjoy a well-made replica from a museum gift shop.

Give her a gift card to her favorite lingerie shop or choose sets in classic white or cream. If you want to give her something in sexy black, try a sleek, satin nightgown that's slit to above the knee.

Your Capricorn girlfriend's man-criteria can be so specialized that you will rarely bump heads over the same guy. Plus, there aren't that many men in the world that she would consider worth fighting over with her best friend.

Speed Bumps

I've never had a humble opinion in my life.
If you're going to have one, why bother to be humble about it?
FOLK SINGER JOAN BAEZ (JANUARY 9)

Sometimes your Capricorn girlfriend can be so busy being realistic that she forgets that you have feelings.

She's interfering. This is different from the well-meant meddling of sister Leo. If Cappy decides that you are too fat, too thin, or that she thinks your guy is no good, she'll sit you down and dump on you in an unceremonious, you-need-to-hear-this way. While you are picking your jaw up off the ground, she'll continue with her plan of what you need to do to correct the situation. Whether you are prepared to listen or even want to hear this information means little to her. This is her Tenth House, Saturn-ruled soul's attempt to play dominant parent. In old astrology, the Tenth House represented the father figure. Today, it can be either sex, but is the parent who controls the family—the one who sets curfew and grounds you when you screw up.

Your Cappy pal may be acting out of concern, but that won't help when she's suddenly surprised you with a one-two punch to your feelings. And like a real parent on a roll, she will be hard to reason with or to shut up. Don't try. Do attempt to understand that she is operating from the point of view of feeling responsible that the truth, no matter how hard to take, is good for you. What she lacks is finesse in dispensing it. After she finishes giving you the brutal facts as she sees them, don't argue. You'll get into a debate you won't win and that will probably end in a shouting match. Capricorns are Cardinal Earth. Her need to be boss runs deep.

Don't thank her, either. You'll open the door to future sermons. Say something like you're sure that she believes she is right and that you know she's trying to be a friend. Then, depending on how harsh she was and how pissed off you are, either change the subject or tell her to drop it.

The first time this happens is the worst. Soon you'll learn to ignore her when she's in this mode, just like you ignored most of those this-is-for-your-own-good lectures from your real parents.

Another version of her soul's need to think it knows best happens when you need her help or advice, but she's only going to give it if you let her take control. Suppose you need help on a project at work. She's happy to help, but only on her terms. This can range from changing the background color of your presentation to questioning your content, even if you are the expert. In this case, thank her for her input, but don't budge. She might tell you that she can't sell your idea the way it stands, so why waste her time if you won't listen. Stand your ground. This is Goat head-bumping. She bumps to see if you're willing to fight as hard as she would for your idea. Do it, but be professional. She'll probably bitch a little more, but she'll help and will respect you for not being a pushover.

One of the worst speed bumps you'll have with a Capricorn chum is intolerance. There is probably at least one thing upon which she's fixated. It could be as simple as your love of sushi, which she finds totally disgusting, or as serious as prejudging people. Anyone who dresses that casually must be a lazy slob. Anyone who likes reality TV is stupid. She can be incapable of understanding why other people don't see the world the way she does. Or that they might not be ambitious as she, or at all. Next time she's on a roll about her favorite pet peeve, try diplomatically bringing it to her attention that not everyone has the same taste or same objective in life. That's why there are so many choices. Most of them are neither bad nor good, just different. She's a smart girl. Once you open her eyes, she might be less likely to go off on a tangent next time. Keep it up. Your Mountain Goat girlfriend learns to lighten up, the same way as she learns everything else, one step at a time.

Romance Rating

I love leather, and it's great to be a bad girl sometimes.
When I'm with Grandma it's flowers and
when I'm out on the town scoping guys, you know . . .
ACTRESS ELIZA DUSHKU (DECEMBER 30)

It's as easy to love a rich man as a poor one. This old joke is often used to sum up your Cappy friend's outlook. Although it's far from what she's really all about, as with every cliché, there's a bit of truth involved.

A Capricorn woman approaches love as she does everything else: slowly, and with the intent of building something solid and lasting. She's probably the least likely sign in the zodiac to believe in love at first sight. This girlfriend can work as hard at finding the right man as she does finding the right career. She'll observe him first, keeping her feelings to herself. Her realistic Saturn soul and Masculine Earth nature want the real deal. She knows that the thrill of first love fades, and she looks for the long-term glow that grows from that first passion. As for a rich man, to her *rich* means a man who is a good provider not only of money, but of trust, support, and constant love.

She's not into gender-specific roles when it comes to creating a future together. Yes, she is chic, glamorous, classy, and can be exceptionally feminine. She also has an inner strength and resolve that's as tough as any guy's. As a Cardinal sign, she likes to take the lead, and she'll try to take the lead in designing their future too. This is where the trouble begins.

Your Cappy chum isn't about to submit to any man in the long run. He often mistakes her reserved approach for shyness, and her willingness to defer to him in the beginning as a sign of submission. Wrong. She's not truly shy. She's assessing him. If he doesn't measure up, she'll dump him and continue her search. If she thinks he's a good prospect, she'll proceed with her usual caution, keeping him at emotional arm's length until she feels comfortable.

At best, she wants to fully partner with her man to build their life together. At worst, she insists on dominating him. As does sister Virgo, this chum wants it both ways: a guy with potential whom she can mold to fit her specifications. This is her first lose-lose situation. If she can push him around, she'll end up with Mr. Yes-dear who's happy to let her call the shots and work herself to death while he skates by assuming less and less responsibility. If she can't push him around, she can get in a duel-to-the-death power struggle. Either way, she ends up alone.

There's another trite saying that can apply to a Cappy chum: "Get them young and train them right." This pattern isn't exclusive to chauvinistic males. It's your Capricorn pal's second lose-lose scenario. Whether it's unconscious or not, she can take the same approach. This isn't the Mommy syndrome that Cancer girls fall into. This is Pygmalion. She dates or marries a younger man, then sets out to dictate both the relationship and his future. Again, the sword cuts both ways, and she can either end up with Pussy-whipped Phil, who is afraid to dress without her approving his choice of suits, or with First Wife's disease. After she spends her time, energy, and money to turn him into her doctor, or lawyer, or high-powered business man, he leaves her—usually for a younger woman.

When that happens, she's not likely to dissolve in hysterics or spend days in a pity party. What she's likely to do is to spend weeks in a depressed funk, refusing to be cheered up, and suffering in self-imposed isolation. She might get argumentative and ask you to leave her the hell alone. Don't. This is when she needs you most. Call regularly. Even if she doesn't pick up for a couple of days, she'll be happy to hear your voice. With a little coaxing you can get her to stick her head out for coffee, or let you visit.

Let her take the lead in talking it out. She's not into spilling her guts about her emotional life, even to you. When she does vent, you're more likely to get an overview versus the blow-by-blow details that some other girlfriends need to unload. She might not bring it up at all. That's okay. Stick to small talk if she wants to. What's important is that you're close and supportive.

Your Capricorn BFF is almost unmatched in her ability to help you when it's your turn to cry. She seems to know exactly what to say and do to make you cheer up. She'll use her considerably wicked sense of humor to make a couple of downright dirty remarks about the jerk who broke your heart, and she'll plan an evening out that is guaranteed to take your mind off of your trouble. She'll also hold your hand and listen to you vent—as long as you don't slip into victim mode. Do that and your little Goat will give you a friendly kick-in-the-butt attitude adjustment.

In romance, as in every other area of her life, a Capricorn woman is like that sure-footed Mountain Goat. She might stumble over a few rocks, or even take a tumble on a sandy slope, but she jumps right back up, shakes herself off, and starts up the mountain again.

Bitch Factor

I do everything for a reason.
Most of the time, the reason is money.
ACTRESS AVA GARDNER (DECEMBER 24)

These misbehaving miscreants will trample your toes and your feelings in their rush to prove that they are superior beings when in reality, they're only clueless blowhards.

Pretentious Pat was born on the wrong side of the tracks and has been trying to pull herself up by everyone else's bootstraps since.

Unfortunately, the only thing self-made about this bad girl is her phony pedigree. She takes the game of one-upmanship to a new high.

If your uncle is a congressman, Pat will say that hers signed the Declaration of Independence. Earn a huge promotion, and she'll tell you that she could have had the job but turned it down. Pat is the poster girl of one-upmanship. She has no qualms about stretching the truth until it's as thin as thawing ice, as long as she can make you think that her blood is bluer or her bank account fatter. She'll put down your taste in clothes, or cars, or men. If you tell her that you're taking a trip to Hawaii, she'll tell you that she's heading for a private island in the South Pacific.

Pat tries to make you and everyone around her believe she's so above the ordinary. Truth is, she's the most common bore in town. Stick a pin in this everlasting windbag and she'll fly around the room backward to land in a hissing heap in the corner.

One step down on the ladder of inverted spiritual success is Ms. Greedy, who wouldn't give a dime to a homeless person if she had a million bucks in the bank. She might be the richest woman in town, but she'll opt for a yard sale rather than send her clothes or worn-out furniture to charity. Ask her to lend you $5 until payday and she'll say she left her wallet at home.

Ms. G.'s frugality has nothing to do with her financial status and everything to do with thinking that she's better than the rest of us. People expect too many handouts. Why should she give her hard-earned money away? Why should she give perfectly good clothing to charity when she could earn a few bucks back on consignment?

Why should you want to even talk to this stingy bitch?

If micromanaging were an Olympic sport, the Tyrant would win the gold medal hands down. The most possessive Taurus or controlling Scorpio looks a rank amateur up against this one. At work, she's the one who's always standing over everyone's shoulder, making sure that anything she's delegated is done precisely, exactly as she directs.

Don't do it and there will be hell to pay. At home, she controls everything from the family diet to who the family can choose as friends to
what everyone watches on TV.

Ms. T. usually surrounds herself with a collection of weak-kneed
losers who all depend upon her to dictate their miserable lives, which
she is only too happy to do. She loves her role and makes sure that
everyone knows how everything would fall apart if it weren't for her
pulling the strings. She's easy to spot because every conversation the
woman has begins with either, "You will do as I say," or "Don't make
me have to tell you twice."

Don't make *me* have to tell you twice to avoid this controlling
bimbo like the plague she is.

Bondability

Sister of the soul: Taurus, Capricorn, Pisces
Inner circle: Virgo, Cancer, Aquarius
Party pal: Gemini, Leo, Sagittarius
Casual chum: Aries, Scorpio, Libra
Famous Capricorn friendship: Kate Moss and Lindsay Lohan
(a Cancer)

Venus in Capricorn

In Capricorn, Venus is calm, cool, and collected. Venus here is serious and cautious with her feelings. She's another chum who isn't into instant bonding of any kind. This is because here, Venus is extremely reserved, even shy, about revealing her feelings. A Capricorn Venus is devoted to her friends. This placement makes the flightiest or most competitive Sun more loyal and dependable.

She's also something of a paradox, because as close as she holds her emotions, this Venus is capable of some of the most outrageous behavior in the zodiac. She can deliberately act up at anytime. *Act* is the key word here, as this girlfriend is totally in control of her emotions, even when she's being over-the-top flirty.

Capricorn Venus is also health conscious as is Virgo Venus. However, hers is a common-sense approach to health and beauty, versus the sometimes hypochondriac motivation of Virgo. Cappy Venus will eat and exercise in moderation to avoid yo-yo diet swings. She instinctively seems to know what works, and any Sun sign benefits from this practical talent.

Her beauty regimen is the same. She'll never forget the sunscreen, even in winter, and her body care products and cosmetics will be ones that are proven to be the best for her skin, even if that means a hefty cost; ditto for her beauty and spa treatments. She'll do the research beforehand, but once she finds the perfect-for-her place to be pampered, she'll be one of its most loyal customers.

This natural instinct for knowing what is best governs her fashion sense as well. Even if she's more of a tomboy than glamour girl, this Venus child has the knack for looking like a fashion plate.

Capricorn Venus does well in any job that requires trust and responsibility. She is often drawn to the banking or investment business and has a knack for finding wealthy partners or patrons to help finance her dreams.

Moon in Capricorn

Every Capricorn Moon has an inner well of reserve and determination that allows her to climb over every obstacle in her path. Here, the emotions are structured, mature, and responsible. Again, this is a paradoxical placement, for these Moon girls can often feel insecure and that they don't fit in anywhere.

According to astrology, this is another difficult position for the emotional Moon. This Moon gives a strong need for control to any Sun sign. Usually, this is self-directed, to keep her emotions and life managed. However, this girlfriend can also attempt to manage your life. Plus she will never hesitate to speak up if she feels you need your chain rattled.

Money is important to this Moon sign. Not for what it buys, but for the status it can bring. Capricorn Moons are extremely status conscious and often feel as if they don't measure up in some way. Earning money helps boost this woman's self-esteem.

Outwardly, this Moon is socially gracious, determined, focused, and usually has a love of learning. She's not prone to hordes of pals, but a few close and trusted comrades with whom she can be herself. Once she is your friend, she's unwavering in her devotion.

Through the Water signs, the Capricorn Moon is said to be auspicious for attracting fame. In the Air signs, it enhances their resourcefulness. Earth signs become even more practical and leader oriented, and Fire signs can be so self-confident that virtually nothing can stop their success.

Your Capricorn Guy Pal

Patient and persevering, a Capricorn buddy knows how to enjoy life. Of all the guys in the zodiac, the phrase "Work hard, play hard" applies to him.

It might take you a little while to win this man's friendship, as he has a built-in resistance to jumping into anything too quickly. Initiate the conversation when you first meet, and if you can make him laugh, or at least chuckle, you'll jump on the inside track. When he opens up, his conversation is more likely to be on a serious subject, so pay attention as though he were the president. Unless he's well under thirty, he's a more traditional kind of guy, so don't spring too many far-out ideas or unconventional theories on him.

His party style ranges from a group trip to Vegas for the weekend to rooting for his team over burgers and beer at the local sports bar. In Vegas he'll probably prefer catching the shows to gambling. Most Capricorn guys like to hang on to their hard-earned cash. He's not into painting the town red all in one night. But he will go out to a new place every night. This guy is all about stamina, and even when he's well past middle age, you can count on your Capricorn buddy to still be your dance partner when most other guys are snoring in their recliners.

He's usually handy around the house, so you can ask his help with everyday repairs. Be sure that you repay him for any parts or supplies. Don't just offer; hand him the money. He might refuse to take it, but Goats can be funny about money, so it's best to be straightforward.

His emotions are steadfast. If he liked you at twenty, you'll still be his buddy at eighty. He'll stand by you through anything and hurt for you when you're upset. He'll give you thoughtful advice if you ask for it and respect your privacy if you don't feel like talking. Under his sometimes tough-guy exterior, he has a heart of gold. Having his friendship is like striking it rich.

Chapter Eleven
Aquarius

January 20–February 18
Element: Air
Quality: Fixed
Symbol: The Water Bearer
Ruler: Saturn and Uranus
Birthstone: Amethyst
Colors: Electric blue, neon hues
Flowers: Iris, orchid
Fragrances: Cherry blossom, myrrh, cedar, incenses

Soul Design

Everyone wants to ride with you in the limo,
but what you need is someone who will
take the bus with you when the limo breaks down.
TALK SHOW HOST OPRAH WINFREY (JANUARY 29)

Friendly.

Independent.

Opinionated.

Your Aquarius BFF is an enigma. Strong willed, opinionated, even defiant, she's also compassionate, liberal, and so easygoing that you may forget she's a *Fixed* sign. Ms. Aquarius combines all these traits, plus the special-to-her trait of doing exactly what she pleases without regard to what anyone else thinks—including you. Understand that, and it's easy to gain her friendship.

Besides, she does it in such a nice way that you might not even notice. This girlfriend is neither mean spirited nor egotistical. As does Pisces, she proceeds at her own pace, doing her own thing, but with more self-direction and less need for approval.

There's a misconception about her element that comes from her symbol, the Water Bearer. Aquarius is not a Water sign. She's *Masculine Fixed Air*. Masculine signs are assertive. Fixed signs can be stubborn and opinionated. She's more pleasant about it than Taurus, more open in discussing it than Scorpio, and less volatile than Leo. However, she's as unlikely to change her mind about a belief or judgment call as any of the others. Being Fixed Air means that this girl can talk about her latest cause until everyone is blue in the face.

The symbolic "water" that pours out of the vessel carried by either the woman or man as she is astrologically portrayed is knowledge. Her symbol, the Water Bearer, is a conduit for the flashes of insight that come from the heavens down to us mortals. When she's in *listen to what I have to say* mode, she's operating from a soul-level need to make you understand the importance of her idea, cause, or opinion. What you think might not matter. What is important is that she delivers the message.

Her soul lives in the Eleventh House of Friends, Groups, Hopes, and Wishes. In its previous pad, the Tenth House of Career, it was concerned with public recognition and what it gained from the world. In the Eleventh House, the goal is what the soul can do *for* the world. On some level your Aquarius pal will be more than a little interested in making her world, your world, or humanity at large a better place.

She's dual-ruled by Saturn and Uranus. Disciplined Saturn gives your Aquarius chum a love of order and tradition. It makes her feel that nothing easily gained can be very good. Saturn equates value with hard work. Rebellious Uranus bestows her need for freedom. To quote an old *Star Trek* line, "The needs of the many outweigh the needs of the few, or the one." You'll see this in her inner circle, among her coworkers, and with her family. *What's best for all of us?*

A caveat here is that, as a Fixed sign, she'll automatically assume that she knows what is best. As with all of your Fixed sign girlfriends, you'll have to prove that your idea is better. Make as logical an argument as you can. She isn't into listening to emotional plea bargaining.

She's probably the most independent girl in the zodiac. She's another girlfriend who doesn't believe in exclusive friendship. Try to pin her down, or act jealous of her other chums, and she's capable of dropping you like a rock.

Your Aquarius girlfriend can be so emotionally detached that she might not stop to think about how her behavior or decision will affect you. Don't be afraid to remind her of your viewpoint. She's not deliberating being bossy. The positive side is her ability to stand outside of any situation and look at it objectively. This makes her another great mediator of issues, as is sister Libra.

Her struggle is that her Uranian nature is in a constant battle of wills with her Saturn side. Uranus is the rugged individualist that rebels against the status quo. Saturn *is* the status quo to a degree. Stay on course. Work hard. Take it one step at a time. This is what causes those periodic rebellions where she shakes things up a little. Maybe she's a brunette and suddenly dyes her hair flaming red or decides at sixty to get her pilot's license. Or she might drop out altogether.

A friend and former coworker of mine is an Aquarius. She's been married to the same guy for forty years, raised six children, endured all the joys and despairs that life dished out, and worked to help support her family at a variety of jobs. She was active in her church and volunteered many of her "spare" hours to visiting members and working in the genealogy office. When I met her she was in her mid-fifties and a model of Saturn's diligence and tradition.

Two years later, after her youngest child was safely on his own, she and her husband sold everything they had, including the family home and its contents, bought a small RV, and hit the road. That was more than five years ago, and today they are still happily dividing their time between Mexico in the winter and Montana during the summer. Although he heartily agreed, the idea to dump tradition and go on a permanent vacation was hers. This is a classic example of Uranus's need for absolute freedom and independence.

Your Aquarius chum is usually fighting for a cause. Unlike Aries, who fights on a personal basis one to one, Aquarius has a larger picture in mind. You might see her working on your local public TV or radio drive, or collecting clothes for charity, or serving soup at a homeless shelter. Not that the other sister signs aren't as giving, but nearly all Aquarians either work overtly or devote part of their time to helping others.

The idealism of Aquarius isn't the flower-child free-love-and-harmony of the '60s, where everyone sits around dreaming and no one does anything. That's Pisces idealism. The dawn of the Age of Aquarius is the dusk of the Age of Pisces.

Aquarius is the idealistic creator. Make a better world. Saturn is the practical worker. Earn it by learning how, then make something useful. An excellent example of Aquarius-as-humanitarian blending with Saturn-as-achiever is Oprah Winfrey. The Oprah Winfrey Leadership Academy for Girls does both. In providing these children with an education, it arms them to effectively make changes to build a better future for themselves and their country and ultimately the world. Every time a person becomes self-sufficient, it helps mankind. For the good of the many. Pure Aquarius.

Your Aquarius friend has a wicked sense of humor and can be a great practical joker. Actress Geena Davis has been quoted as saying, "I have an elbow that bends the wrong way, and I'd do things like stand in an elevator and the doors would close, and I'd pretend that my arm had got caught in it, and then I'd scream, 'Ow, ow, put it back!'" While your friend might not go to this length to get a laugh, she is sure to have a somewhat skewed perspective about what's funny. She won't care if anyone else laughs as long as she does. Even if she gets a little over the top, she's never boring.

She also loves to shake up a dull conversation or person with an offhand remark that sounds innocent but is designed to provoke. Shoot her a disapproving look and she'll give you a wide-eyed stare. "Did I say something wrong?"

She'll have an eclectic group of friends, as do sisters Gemini and Sagittarius. However, an Aquarius pal usually keeps her friendship groups separate. You may never meet any of them. It's a quirk of hers. She likes knowing that she can quilt for the poor every Thursday with the church group and study astrology every Saturday at the local New Age center. She doesn't feel compelled to share that knowledge. Don't mistake her action for either embarrassment or guilt. She easily mixes with people from all walks of life, but understands that doesn't apply to everyone, so she is considerate of the feelings and beliefs of each of her friendship circles. In her opinion, it's also no one else's business.

Her personal style can be as eclectic as her various groups of pals. She might mix and match clothing styles or wear exotic, handmade jewelry. She's likely to be environmentally conscious, and if she's an older Water Bearer, probably was before it became fashionable.

She can be a celebrity watcher. She's fascinated with people and likes to try to figure out what makes them tick. She has her own peculiar way of scrutinizing them too. More like a scientist observing a bug under a microscope than getting emotionally involved on a raving fan level.

An Aquarius pal prides herself on not blindly following the pack or agreeing with the safest point of view. Yes, she can get stubborn. Yes, she'll stir the pot just to watch your reaction. She's also one of the most tolerant girlfriends in the Universe, and believes in live and let live. She's quirky. She marches to her own life beat and doesn't care what others think. The one certain thing you can count on with her is that you never know quite what to expect. That's why she's so much fun.

Groove Meter

Considering how dangerous everything is,
nothing is really frightening.
AUTHOR GERTRUDE STEIN (FEBRUARY 3)

An Aquarius woman was born under the sign of friendship. You won't find her sitting at home when she can play, and whatever you decide to do, she'll have fun. She's as adventurous as sister Sagittarius, as chatty as Gemini, and as outgoing as Leo.

She's also up for anything that is unique or off the beaten path. She loves going where she's never been and doesn't know anyone. It gives her the opportunity to observe the locals and make new friends.

An Aquarius girl and serendipity seem to go hand in hand. When you're on a road trip, she'll suddenly decide to turn left instead of right and you could end up in an out-of-the-way place full of shop-till-you-drop treasures. When that happens, she's having flashes of

Uranus's insight. When she skews off the trail, follow her and you'll end up having a better time than if you'd stuck to your original plan.

The same theory applies to group outings. Although she enjoys the usual girls' night out, ask her along to your next astronomy club meeting to watch the stars or invite her to go with you to the planetarium. Heading for a lecture on UFOs or an exotic food tasting? She'll happily tag along. Or simply invite her over for popcorn and a sci-fi or fantasy flicks night.

This pal loves to shop online. She can buy clothes, books, a new gadget, or anything her heart desires, all in an instant. And she prefers the new versus the old. She's not the girl to take antique shopping or to a vintage clothing store, even though the retro look might be her style. This girlfriend is always up to date on the latest fashion trends. She'll have fun at the mall, but will most likely have a few favorite boutiques that specialize in unusual or original designs, such as saris from India or wooden shoes from Holland. They won't necessarily be expensive, just different. She likes to set herself apart from the crowd.

If she's athletic, invite her to go cross-country skiing or mountain climbing. Set up a doubles tennis match or miniature golf tournament. She'll also sail around the world with you or go along when you visit your relatives in another country.

Uranus's need to keep things exciting can make her an adrenaline junkie. Her idea of a petting zoo might include patting a crocodile on the head. She might think it's cool to hike across a suspension bridge high above a raging river.

An Aquarius girlfriend of mine is hooked on being scared. Her favorite theme parks are the ones with gigantic roller coasters and freefall drops that make you think you might die. She loves movies, from horror to psychological thrillers that make her skin crawl or be temporarily afraid of the dark. On Halloween, her favorite place is a local fright maze set up in a California vineyard with little light and lots of live "monsters" that spring at her out of the night to make her scream.

Yours might not be quite the thrill seeker, but she will have a wonderful talent for surprising you with imaginative adventures.

Use your imagination when you're planning a party for her. She'll love a surprise and isn't fussy about the details. Have an indoor picnic and roast marshmallows in the fireplace. Take her to the midnight opening of a new movie, then out for a birthday breakfast afterward.

She likes one-of-a-kind gifts. If you're the creative type and can make her a piece of original jewelry or a flowing skirt in her favorite colors, she'll adore it. She's also into the latest technology and will like a gift card to the electronics store so that she can find some cutting-edge gadget to help simplify her life.

She loves a challenge. Give her a book of mind-bending word puzzles or the latest version of a complicated video game. She'll enjoy reading true crime stories or fast-paced thriller novels. She also might like books on New Age topics or subjects that deal with unexplained phenomena such as crop circles or mass disappearances throughout history.

Her bridal shower should be as much fun. Rent a limo and cruise around town while she drinks champagne and opens her gifts, then stop at her favorite restaurant for brunch or dinner. If you're celebrating at someone's home, flip on the shopping channel and tell her she can buy anything she wants up to a preset amount, or make the same offer of an Internet mini-spree.

An Aquarius friend has eclectic tastes. Buy her a set of multicolored glassware in iridescent blues and greens. She'll like a slow cooker so that dinner's ready the minute she walks in the door, as well as any time-saving kitchen gadget. She might like an African tribal mask or a neon-lighted wall clock. Appeal to her Saturn side with a comfort food recipe book or a towel warmer for her bath.

Adult board games will be fun for her and her man. Give her a satin nightshirt with matching short gown, or an assortment of colored thongs decorated with lace, beads, or rhinestones.

She's fun, funny, and full of life. Your Aquarius girlfriend thrives on friendship, and with her as a pal the adventures never stop.

Speed Bumps

Did you hear what I said? It was very profound.
DR. LAURA SCHLESSINGER (JANUARY 16)

Aquarius Air is Fixed, which means that your Water Bearer girlfriend can sometimes be stubborn and very opinionated. She can get an idea in her head that she won't let go of, or say one thing, then turn around and do the opposite. Or expect you to listen to a dissertation on her new favorite cause and shut you down if you dare to disagree.

She gets do-as-I-say-not-as-I-do syndrome. This irritating trait is when she lectures you because you got wasted twice in a week, or have gained a few pounds, or are having a fling with a bad boy. When you point out that she was as drunk as you were, that she's gained two pounds more than you, and that her bad boy is married, she'll go off like a rocket. Your Aquarius chum doesn't know how phony she sounds. When you point it out, she may be shocked at herself, but she might yell at you anyway. Feel free to yell back. This is one girl in the zodiac that you can argue with without fear of losing her friendship.

An Aquarius chum can be one of the most self-absorbed women on Earth. Never mind your Aries pal's need for attention, or a Leo chum's attempt to grab the spotlight. When a Water Bearer is in self-centered mode, she gets irrational. She demands your time, your help, your agreement with everything she says. She wants you to follow her lead or take her advice without question, and if you don't, you'll suffer a tirade.

Turn the tables and ask her for help, time, or blind loyalty and she'll squeal that you're taking advantage of her good nature. You always take advantage. Everyone always takes advantage. She thinks she's being logical and won't understand when you tell her she's being unreasonable. This behavior is usually due to her periodic need to stand out. She is so good at being a team player and going along with the crowd that she begins to feel very unspecial. She'd like to be in the spotlight sometimes, but can give herself a guilt trip if she demands her way. She's all about the group, not necessarily the individual. So she blows when she thinks the group is preying on her goodwill.

The cure is simple. Ask for a timeout and ask her what's really bothering her. Once she vents the true issue, she and you will both feel better.

Follow up with simple praise. Yes, she is the best friend in the Universe. You don't know how you would get along without her. It works wonders. An Aquarius girl presents a picture of cool confidence and cheerful helpfulness. She doesn't allow herself the luxury of a pity party very often. Because of these traits we can overlook the fact that, inside, she can be as vulnerable as the rest of us.

An irritating but harmless speed bump is her ability to climb on her soapbox without warning and trap you into listening to chatter about her latest cause. You'll hear about its history, purpose, and financial resources, plus several case histories proving why this is the most deserving organization in the Universe. Don't ask her about last week's cause, it's already forgotten. If she isn't expounding on an aid organization, she'll be telling you how she's taken someone under her wing to help straighten out her life. If this is a mutual friend, she might ask your help. She might also ask you to contribute time or money to the charity.

She does this when you're at lunch or on a road trip or somewhere she's sure that you're her captive audience. You've heard it all before, and you'll hear it all again. She was born to make things better. So grit your teeth a little if you have to and cough up a few bucks or hours to chip in. After all at least this girlfriend is trying to give something back to the world, and that's a good thing.

When your Aquarius pal gets on her high horse, she can swing from mildly annoying to full-blown aggravating. She can drive you mad with her endless declarations of how the world should run, and irk you when she decides you need an attitude adjustment but fails to see her own bad behavior. She's also capable of the most selfless friendship in the zodiac and is definitely the BFF who will be happy to ride with you in either the limo or the bus.

Romance Rating

Some people go to priests; others to poetry; I to my friends.
AUTHOR VIRGINIA WOOLF (JANUARY 25)

An Aquarius woman is born liberated. She's funny, usually brainy, and sexy without the ballsy style of some of her sisters around the zodiac. She has a powerful romantic streak. She wants a guy who's both friend and lover, one who can bend her mind as well as her body. All she asks is that he respect her as a person and not try to stifle her need to join a few causes or play with her pals. If he doesn't comply, she won't notice because she'll already be on her way out the door to a women's rights meeting.

The love danger for your Water Bearer chum is that she can live so much in her own head that she never understands what is going on in her guy's. She's not into Mars-Venus role play. She believes in an equal partnership and is willing to pull her weight in the relationship, as Capricorn does. The difference is that Cappy tries to control, and your Aquarius pal assumes everyone is on the same wavelength. However, she never bothers to check. She can be so detached that she misses the signals that something is wrong.

It can be difficult for her to express her deeper feelings, and she's not a girl who goes for sappy sentiment. Yet, she often falls for a guy who seethes with passion, temper, or is emotionally needy. At first, she adores the attention, and he adores being the one to unleash her considerable emotions. Later, she moves back into remote-ville and he begins to feel like a body that she may or may not be interested in any longer.

From her viewpoint, once she's committed herself to the relationship or marriage, that should be that. She comes home every night. She's faithful. She's loyal. She's neither jealous nor clingy. What more can he want?

One day she'll find out when she wakes up—too late—to realize that he's been snagged by a woman who is neither as cute nor smart as she is, but who simply paid more attention to the poor slob. She'll never see it coming either, and when it happens, she'll be devastated.

She'll want to get her mind off the mess, so gather your crew and take her out clubbing. She can bounce back as fast as she fell, which is good. However, she will probably never truly understand what happened.

When you're the one who gets dumped, she'll listen to you cry, but not for long. She can't deal too well with raw emotion, and although she cares about you, she's as likely to cringe when you're sobbing as to offer you a hug. She will let you rant and rave; that she can understand. She'll also insist that you blow your nose and come out to play. She knows that nothing is better than to hang with your friends, and she'll be right.

When you are scoping out guys together, and you spot a cutie you'd like to know better, don't worry about your Aquarius pal trying to move in first. She's not only a fair player with her friends, she's probably already involved in a debate over the next election with the hothead on the next bar stool.

Bitch Factor

One likes people much better when they're
battered down by . . . misfortune than when they triumph.
AUTHOR VIRGINIA WOOLF (JANUARY 25)

Bad-girl Water Bearers aren't truly evil; they're just an obnoxious bunch of blathering bores.

At first, you'll think that Self-sacrificing Sally is one of the most admirable women you've ever met. She always puts her family first. She's a hard worker who is willing to go without in order to sock money away for both her kids' educations. She supports her husband's hobbies.

From whom do you hear these glowing reports? Sally. Who else? If you observe her closely, you'll notice that she's wound tighter than a cheap watch spring. Sally's repressed every Aquarian instinct of independence, and the only way that she can let some of her aggression out and not feel guilty is to let you know how taken advantage of she is, but by couching it as selfless love for her family.

Although you might feel sorry for her, there's nothing that you can do except inch away until you're at a safe distance. Sooner or later, this one will blow, and when she does, the explosion will be nuclear.

The Meddler has such a boring life that she resorts to gossip to keep herself entertained. She likes to create mischief by engineering little feuds, then stand back and watch the mayhem. She's the phony friend who tries to get you to diss one of your other chums while she's gathering tidbits about you from someone else. Then she spills everything to everyone in order to entertain herself. You'll usually find this one operating at full speed in the office and moving from cubicle to cubicle, coffee cup in hand and a cheerful grin on her face.

The only thing you have to do is keep your mouth shut around her and watch what happens when the rest of your coworkers get wise to her. It won't take long until Ms. M. is kicked out of the grapevine club and left sitting in a corner talking to herself.

Last and worst is the in-your-face Verbal Hurricane who thinks she knows it all. She'll assume the role of therapist and not hesitate to tell you what she thinks is wrong with you and how you should fix yourself. Balk at her rude behavior and you'll start to feel like a frog in a blender. She's right. She's justified. She's a self-righteous fanatic.

V-H girl is the coworker who makes the rounds spewing her latest conspiracy theory, or political or moral viewpoints. She's the mother who berates her children for having ideas that don't coincide with hers.

If she acts like she wants to be friends with you, it's because she feels you should have the benefit of her knowledge and expertise. Only she's usually dumber than dirt and her only expertise is talking so loud and long that people give in just to shut her up.

Don't let this one start with you. The best way to handle her is to learn the three things she absolutely hates the most, then pounce on her first. Tell her you're only trying to enlighten her with the real truth. This might actually shock her into silence, for which you will get a standing ovation from her other weary victims.

Bondability

Sister of the soul: Gemini, Libra, Sagittarius
Inner circle: Aries, Capricorn, Pisces
Party pal: Aquarius, Taurus, Virgo
Casual chum: Cancer, Leo, Scorpio
Famous Aquarius friendship: Oprah Winfrey and Gayle King (a Capricorn)

Venus in Aquarius

Venus in Aquarius gives every Sun sign a popular edge in making friends. Here Venus is rarely jealous, never possessive, and always nonjudgmental. No matter what her Sun sign is, an Aquarius Venus chum sets her own rules and usually doesn't care what is or isn't socially acceptable. She follows her own path, even in love, and appreciates friendship as much as romance in her affairs.

Her talents lie in working with the public, and she often will have a futuristic outlook that can make her a predictor of fashion, art, or technological trends.

Aquarius Venus is either on or off when it comes to making friends, as well as falling in love. This girl either likes you or isn't interested, and she'll usually decide within the first few minutes after you've met.

Aquarius Venus also sets her own beauty standards. She's another woman who follows the latest trends, but she leans toward techno-gadgets that will firm her facial muscles and massage creams that "dissolve" fat under the skin. She'll try and discard as many new products as she can afford to experiment with. Venus here loves shimmering body powder, sparkly eye shadows, and super-shiny lipsticks.

Her fashion sense is eclectic. Whether it's a collection of running shoes in neon colors, or unusual jewelry from around the world, the most conservative-dressing Sun sign will always have at least one area in which her Aquarius Venus will manifest her sense of original and edgy flair.

Aquarius in Venus is considered a lucky placement for realizing one's hopes and wishes.

Moon in Aquarius

An Aquarius Moon is idealistic, honest, and well balanced. Of all the Moon signs, this girlfriend is the least likely to lose her head in a crisis. This is another favorable position for the emotional Moon, as Aquarius adds a detached, rational aspect to even the most sensitive, sensual Sun.

The Aquarius Moon is expressive, funny, observant, and outgoing. This girlfriend is interested in your life as well as the lives of everyone she knows. She's also interested in the unusual and can be a bit emotionally eccentric in her choice of friends and lovers. No matter what her Sun sign is, this girlfriend rarely becomes so emotionally connected that she loses herself in another person.

Your Aquarius Moon girlfriend is close without being cloying. She's undemanding and won't expect you to be at her beck and call. She won't be at yours either. She seeks a balance between commitment and independence. This Moon adds the Aquarian traits of intelligence and individualism to any Sun sign.

In the Air signs, this Moon strengthens the ability to communicate and get along with anyone. It adds originality and flair to the practical talents of the Earth signs and makes the exuberant Fire signs even more forceful and magnetic. In Water, the Aquarius Moon bestows a unique ability for finding original ways to express traditional ideas.

Your Aquarius Guy Pal

He's a maverick. Your Aquarius buddy thrives on excitement and change. He makes friends wherever he goes, and each one, including you, is special to him in a unique way. He's another guy that you might not see on a regular basis, but he's so spontaneous that if you invite him to a last-minute party, he'll love to go.

He's a great conversationalist who has definite ideas on everything from politics to the latest conspiracy theory. He's happy to expound on any of the subjects he's interested in, so be a good listener, ask lots of questions, and you'll see him a little more often than his other pals. He's attracted to the strange and unusual, so if you're a girl who likes to watch cable TV shows such as the *World's Worst Medical Conditions,* or *Cannibal Lifestyles,* he's the guy to call. Call him too, when you're on your way to volunteer at the local homeless shelter, a lecture on global warming, or the planetarium.

He's good at giving advice because of his objective outlook. He's not good at handling emotional scenes, so if you need his shoulder, make sure it's to bounce alternatives off of, not to cry on. However, he won't hesitate to defend your honor, even if the other guy is bigger.

Even when he's busy elsewhere, he'll keep in touch by email. He likes technology, and will probably know how to repair and upgrade your PC or laptop. This guy understands stereo instructions and knows how to hook up your DVD player or game system. After he's done, challenge him to a tournament.

Your Aquarius buddy is devoted, friendly, and always ready to play. He's also aware, curious, and has a social conscious. That's about as perfect as it gets.

Chapter Twelve
Pisces

February 19–March 20
Element: Water
Quality: Mutable
Symbol: The Fishes
Ruler: Neptune
Birthstone: Aquamarine
Colors: Sea green, gray-blue
Flowers: Crocus, water lily, jonquil, poppy
Fragrances: Green tea, ginger, linen, musk

Soul Design

Reality is something that you rise above.
SINGER/ACTRESS LIZA MINNELLI (MARCH 12)

Compassionate.

Procrastinating.

Impressionable.

Part wise woman, part naïve child, your Pisces BFF is neither as hedonistic nor as helpless as some horoscopes paint her. She's a contradictory mix of rowdy and reclusive. She may not always want to party with you, but you can always count on her in a crisis. On the surface she's funny, friendly, and fits into any social scene. To win her forever friendship, you have to get by her internal radar.

How do you manage that? Don't try to fool her. In the first place, it's unlikely that you can hide your inner nature from her. According to reincarnation, your Pisces girlfriend has lived many lives, which gives her a special, sometimes uncanny ability to quickly assess a person. Second, there's no need to try to impress her because she accepts people as they are, warts and all. Ever have the feeling that your Pisces girlfriend is looking into you instead of at you? She is.

Most Pisces pals have an active sixth sense. If you introduce a newcomer into your friendship circle and she gets unusually quiet, it's a safe bet that something's pushed her internal warning button. She might not be able to tell you why she feels uncomfortable, which can be exasperating if you are a literal Earth sign or a need-some-facts Air sign. Yet, more often than not, she'll be right. Want a second opinion on the cute guy you want to make a run on? Ask her.

Your Pisces girlfriend is the last sign of the zodiac. She's *Feminine Mutable Water* and ruled by Neptune, the planet of illusion, where all is not what it seems. On the surface she's so easygoing. Under that laid-back exterior, her mind never stops clicking.

Her soul dwells in the Twelfth House, where dreams and reality mix. Words associated with the Twelfth House are *secrets, escapism, karma,* and *psychic powers.* Having moved here from the outgoing Eleventh House, the soul completes its journey around the zodiac. It contains lessons learned from every other sign and House, and for better or worse, is more concerned with how it thinks things should be than with reality. Consciously or unconsciously, a Pisces connects on a different plane than the rest of us. Intuition is as real to her as fact. This ability to tune in to the undercurrents at work, or with her friends, or relatives sometimes puts her on sensory overload.

This is why Twelfth House souls need periodic retreats, and the older your Pisces girlfriend is the more you'll find that to be true. This is different from Taurus's need for R&R after a burst of energy, Cancer's retreat into protection mode, or Scorpio's shutting out of things that upset her. Pisces retreats from life because she can absorb too much of its energy. She also enjoys solitude, for that's when she lets her vivid imagination run wild.

Astrologers often point out that Pisces can have a problem dealing with reality. With Neptune ruling her innerscape, she has a rich fantasy life, which living in the mystical Twelfth House compounds. If you've read one astrology book, you've heard of her penchant for substance abuse and actual departures from reality. Yes, they are a danger for this sign. Fortunately, the extent of your average Fish friend's escapism is into harmless daydreams about the perfect life or lover.

The portrayal of her symbol of the two Fishes, as one swimming to the top of life and the other to the bottom, suggests that she either succeeds or succumbs to life. While self-deception is a real danger, this description isn't as black and white as it appears. She has one foot rooted in Earth's material existence and the other in the spiritual world. This doesn't mean every Pisces is a religious fanatic, or even attends regular church services. But she will be attuned to a higher purpose and probably be on an active search for it in her own life.

She has a style all her own. Whether she's into timeless fashion or follows the fads, your Pisces chum will usually add an elaborate touch to her clothes. Maybe she wears huge, bold jewelry or has a collection of flowing scarves. Whatever it is, chances are she will add flair to her wardrobe that makes her stand out. She'll help you put together a special outfit for a dream date or a night out with the girls. She's loved to play dress-up since she was a little girl, and will happily spend hours helping you shop for clothes and just the right accessories.

She's forgiving. She is not the clueless pushover that she's been painted. Act thoughtlessly, and she might choose to ignore your bad behavior, but don't think that she doesn't understand your motivations. She does. Push her too much and, while she probably won't end the friendship, she will put a healthy-for-her emotional distance between you. Expect her to play the fool, and she'll disappear as quickly as a real fish diving into deeper water.

Ever notice how she can chat for hours with you, but virtually clam up around anyone else, even the other girls in your social circle? It's a twofold reason. First, Pisces are as private as Scorpios, though they don't project the guarded persona. Very few people have her total confidence, and even if you are her best soulmate pal, you won't know everything about this woman. Second, a Pisces chum gathers information by listening. She'll know more about you in a shorter time, as Gemini can. But, her conversational style is to encourage you to talk by her nonverbal smile, nod, and the occasional pertinent question. You might think she's zoned out, but then she'll zap you with an insightful remark that cuts to the core of an issue.

A Pisces girlfriend of mine laughs that she seems to have an invisible the-doctor-is-in sign around her neck. Whether she's listening to a stranger's life story while waiting in the checkout line, or counseling her boss on his next career move, people seem to line up to tell her their life stories. She's in demand with friends and family too. It isn't really such a mystery when you understand that she isn't only listening, she's hearing them.

She's nearly shockproof. On the other hand, she might shock you with language so blue it could make a sailor blush, a bawdy observation about someone, or a matter-of-fact discussion about any topic under the Sun. That's the worldly side of her nature, and she has one. Think of Dr. Sue Johansen and her sex talk TV show. A Pisces pal can be as witty as Gemini spouting one-liners and as slapstick funny as a Sagittarius clowning at her own expense.

As is her opposite sign, Virgo, your Pisces can be super-health conscious. This isn't the same as the hypochondriac tendency of Virgo. A Pisces pal's respect for health arises because she can be all too familiar with the consequences of excess. One of the dangers of being all Water is that she often has no boundaries. The Crab is anchored to either the seashore or the bottom of the ocean. The Scorpion is actually a desert creature. Only the Fish moves unrestricted. This can result in an unrestricted appetite for food, drink, sex, or partying. Fortunately, most Pisces don't live up to the bleak expectations that astrology sometimes assigns them. But I'll bet that, at one time or another, your Pisces chum has had a run-in with some sort of overindulgence.

That's why she's a great source of inspiration and information should you be on a trek to get in shape, lose weight, or tackle a more serious health issue. Just don't ask this girlfriend to sweat at the gym. It's not that she hates exercise. She loves to move her body. But she'd rather do it on the dance floor, in the pool, or in a yoga class.

She appreciates honesty. If she solicits your opinion, she wants the truth as you see it. Tell her straightforwardly, but kindly. She sees through brutal observations disguised as truth telling, and she wouldn't do that to you. She's not into dispensing unsolicited advice. She will offer you her insight if you ask. She's likely to have alternative solutions or pinpoint a hidden agenda item that you haven't thought of or recognized in yourself. Her ability to cut to the chase is sometimes amazing.

She's unlikely to be aggressive or full of win-at-any-cost ambitions, which could lead you to believe she's either lazy or too laid-back to have fun with. Not true. She's another sign that's willing to try almost anything once. Because of creative Neptune's influence, she's a natural to invite to any artistic event, from an outdoor concert to the latest modern art exhibit.

Your Pisces pal embraces aging as another unfolding adventure. Born with an old soul, she might not fully realize her potential until midlife. Like Gemini and Virgo, she keeps the illusion of youth well past middle age. When other girlfriends have settled into a comfortable routine, the Fish will make another lifestyle change and keep marching to her own tune. She'll also believe in you when you don't believe in yourself, and supply you with unconditional love and support.

Groove Meter

I've tried to be as eclectic as I possibly can . . .
and so far it's been pretty fun.
ACTRESS HOLLY HUNTER (MARCH 20)

A Pisces girlfriend loves variety, and her style swings from blowout bashes to quiet dinners with her closest friends. Her Mutable Water nature makes it easy for her to mingle at a neighborhood potluck or shake her booty at a rock concert. She'll hang out at your place reading fashion magazines or help you to spend the day checking out the hard bodies around the pool.

She loves to get lost in a movie. Anything will appeal, from comedies to action flicks, with happy endings and illusion-filled adventures usually being her favorites. Want to catch the latest sappy chick flick, fantasy, or animated feature? Ask her along. A Pisces friend of mine puts it this way, "I live with reality. When I go to the movies, I want to forget the world and be entertained." That remark also applies to any social situation. Remember this when you're thinking up something to do. Ballet, any type of music concert, from jazz to classical, and glittery social events appeal to her. So does the flash of a girls-only getaway to Las Vegas.

She likes to make dates. Although she can be spontaneous, she prefers to plan ahead because it gives her time to play dress-up in her closet. Every Pisces pal will try on several outfits, mix and match the accessories, and give herself a fashion show in the mirror before she decides on the one that will look just right for the occasion. Doesn't matter whether it's formal, sporty, or burgers at the corner bar, she sets her mood with her outward appearance. This isn't an ego thing. If she's comfortable with how she looks, then it's easier for her to handle crowds and excitement. Of all the signs, Pisces is the most sensitive to other people's moods and the easiest to succumb to them. To her, wearing the right clothes is like putting on protective armor.

She has a chameleon's ability to blend into any scene. She can get as down and dirty as an Aries on a girls-gone-wild night, or match the elegance of the chicest Capricorn. She can melt into the background so that you lose track of her at a party. So if she disappears, don't worry about it; she'll float back. If she gets crazy, watch her back. It's that no-boundaries thing. Sometimes this girlfriend doesn't know when to quit. She'll also protect and defend you from yourself, or anyone else, when you're out. If you want to go a little wild, you can trust her to stay in control.

Since she rarely steps into the spotlight on her own, if you shine it on her with a party in her honor, she'll be thrilled. If it's her birthday, she'll love to drag it out as long as possible with a party one night, lunch with her coworkers the next day, dinner with the family the next. She can take or leave a surprise party. This is one girlfriend who won't drop hints that her big day is coming up, so the fact that you remembered makes it even more special.

Birthday cards can be any type, from sentimental to sinful. She'll laugh at a gag gift, and she'll love brightly colored socks to keep her feet warm. Buy her gifts that appeal to her spiritual side, such as the latest inspirational CD or book. She likes earrings that complement the color of her eyes or a piece of antique or original jewelry. It doesn't have to be expensive. It should be something that you don't see on every other girl in town.

If it's her bridal shower, think romance versus practical. She'll love soft cotton or silk pillow cases, or a massage at a local day spa to soothe her prewedding nerves. If it's something for her new home, try a blooming plant or cozy lap blanket big enough for two.

Pisces girls have lower energy levels, so where a Fire sign friend might be ready to go all night and an Air sign friend go out every night, whether or not your Fish friend does depends on how tired she is at the moment. If she's stressed, you might have to nag a bit to get her out of the house so she can relax. Once she's there, she'll forget whatever's bugging her and be happy you made her go.

Speed Bumps

I have no idea where I'm going. I would just like to be happy.
ACTRESS BETTY HUTTON (FEBRUARY 26)

Pisces Water goes with the flow. This is an old cliché, but it's one of this girlfriend's best traits. It's also her weakest one. You may feel like tearing your hair, and hers, out if you hear her say, "I don't care what we do," one more time. This isn't because she's incapable of making a decision. She's not into trying to run the show either overtly or from behind the scenes. Her soul operates on a different plane than the rest of us, and mundane things like where you're going for dinner truly aren't important to her. What is important is that she's with friends.

That doesn't help when you're sick of being the one to always arrange the outings. The best way to handle it is to make a simple statement that it's her turn to plan the evening. Whatever she comes up with is sure to be fun.

She's inconsistent. A Pisces woman can think something is brilliant one minute and change her mind the next. She can back out of a trip or evening out as fast. Don't confuse this with Gemini's overbooked calendar. Your Pisces chum has simply changed her mind, and she often changes it a lot. She might get home from work and decide she's too tired to get dressed and meet you at the club. She might talk herself out of a weekend getaway because she's afraid she can't afford it, or has convinced herself that she really doesn't want to be trapped in a car with three or four other girls for that long. As infuriating as this behavior can be, it has nothing to do with you. She's operating from her tendency to take the easy road. When she's tired, or uncertain, the easiest choice is to do nothing.

How do you handle this? The first time it happens, let her know that you're disappointed, but act understanding. The next time it happens, feel free to get a little pushy. If you are really close, playing on her guilt complex is good. Tell her you were depending on her. That usually works because she likes to hear that she's needed. The good news is that most Pisces women don't make this bump a habit. On the contrary, most will go the extra mile, even when they know better.

An issue with your reality-challenged Pisces friend is that this girl can get so caught up in fantasizing about her dreams that she never accomplishes them. This is when she imagines the perfect career, life, happy ending but spends little or no effort on planning. Many Pisces know what they want but have trouble translating that into concrete steps of how to achieve it. You can help by listening and assisting her in assessing her options. It's good if you give her practical advice. Help her to set daily goals, or make a timetable so that she can prove to herself it's doable.

She's negative. All Water signs are moody. Cancer can experience several mood swings in one day. Scorpio sulks about whatever caused her pain or anger. Pisces thinks the whole world is falling apart. If she's on a nothing's-right tangent, she'll bitch about anything from her bad hair day to the price of gas to the latest political scandal. She also goes into nobody-loves-me mode. Even if she's your best friend, listening to her vent for an hour or plowing through a three-page email is bound to try your patience. But try to hang in with her. When she gets in this mood it's usually because she's on the sensory overload I described earlier and she hasn't been able to take a break to rejuvenate. The best thing you can to for her is to distract her with some positive news. Compliment her on hanging in there, or tell her a funny story. Remember she's changeable. Sometimes it's just that easy to make her smile again.

You'll occasionally think that she's lost her mind or that your Pisces BFF isn't from the same planet as the rest of us. Her personality is kind of like the tide. Now she's here, now she's not.

Romance Rating

A friend will tell you that she saw your old boyfriend—
and he's a priest.
WRITER ERMA BOMBECK (FEBRUARY 21)

From the time puberty arrives, your Pisces pal never stops looking for True Love. If she's lucky, and a bit smarter than the average Fish, she might find her soulmate early in life and settle down to live happily ever after. Most likely, she'll kiss a series of toads, marry and divorce one or three, before she realizes that nothing can be perfect. This doesn't mean that she'll necessarily settle, although some Fish do. It means that, like Gemini, Aries, and Libra, it can take her awhile to learn the difference between lust and love.

She wants the fairytale romance. Unlike Virgo, who secretly yearns for a white knight but understands that the concept isn't real, your Pisces pal can get so caught up in the ideal that she ruins her own happiness. When reality strikes, she can have a terrible time coping. Her instinct is to disappear. However, she can decide that she must try to stick it out. In this case, especially if she's married with children, she can emotionally disappear. Her body goes through the motions. Her mind is back in True Love fantasy land.

A married Pisces chum has the ability to divide her life with a lover, as do many men. She can carry on an affair for decades without anyone knowing, including you. Of course, this resolves nothing. She's one woman who can separate her day-to-day commitment to her family from her love affair with the man she's made into that dreamy ideal. This is Pisces escapism at its worst. If she fractures herself this way, there isn't much you can do until she figures it out. The good news is that most Pisces women eventually will. The bad news is that it's usually after the affair has become as disillusioning as the marriage.

However, your average Pisces pal will be much less likely to either stay in a bad relationship or stray. But her penchant is definitely to idolize any guy that she's falling for. Although we all tend to do this in the throes of new passion, a Pisces friend can be totally unrealistic in love. She wants to believe in the ideal so badly that she can be vulnerable to an endless line of lying losers.

When she does get her heart broken, she'll need to lean on you. Don't rationalize, patronize, or scold her. She's already done all of those things to herself. This girl can carry a terrible guilt complex and assume that everything is her fault. Even if the guy was the worst man alive, and she knew it, she'll beat herself up that she should have known better. She's not being a martyr. She's likely to have gone against her intuition in dating the guy in the first place and feels a little embarrassed at herself for doing what she counsels you and everyone else not to do.

Once she's finished with a guy, even though it's taken months or years to dump him, this girl is finished for good. Not only does she not want to see him again, she'll probably act as if he no longer exists. Unlike Aries or Gemini, she has no desire to remain friends. Unlike Scorpio and Cancer, she isn't interested in whether he's suffering without her. She figures that she gave it her all while it lasted, so it's ridiculous to waste any more of her life or emotions on the jerk. When she's reached this point she'll gladly live alone rather than be trapped a second longer.

Think of Elizabeth Taylor and Liza Minnelli. Both of these stars have been married multiple times. How many times have you seen either one of them cozied up to an ex, or including him in her extended family, as have some other stars?

If you're suffering, there's no more compassionate friend than your Pisces chum. She'll hold you if you're sobbing and help you shred your ex's pictures if you're raging. She'll take you away for the weekend to get your mind off the blowup or be your designated driver if you want to get drunk. She's not into judging, so if you decide to take him back, she won't try to talk you out of it, even if she thinks it's a lost cause.

You don't have to worry about her competing with you for the cutie you both spotted on the dance floor. Part of the reason is that, if you're both on the prowl, she'll speak up if she's attracted to him. Plus, it isn't her style to be aggressive in love, so she's not into making ballsy first moves. If she's smitten but shy, you might have to give her a friendly shove to get her to walk up and introduce herself.

Bitch Factor

The problem with people who have no vices is that generally you can be pretty sure that they are going to have some pretty annoying virtues.
MOVIE STAR ELIZABETH TAYLOR (FEBRUARY 27)

Unenlightened Pisces women range from vapid to vicious. Her downside is that she can either become the perpetual victim or a victim-seeking perp.

Substitute Bobblehead Betsy for the wiggly toy that sits on the dashboard of your car and no one would be the wiser. This woman has one opinion. Yours. With her fixed smile and nodding noggin she seems like the perfect friend. She listens to you. She's willing to do anything for you. Or you'll think, until you realize that there's nothing behind those shiny white teeth. Betsy is the human equivalent of all those silly one-liners such as *Her elevator doesn't go all the way to the top* and *She's one bubble off plumb.*

Like the classic cartoon character nearsighted Mr. Magoo, Betsy stumbles through life managing to escape the mishaps herself but leaving behind a wake of disasters. Ask her to help with a project and she'll bobble her eagerness to assist. Leave her alone with the work and she'll sit and stare out the window, forgetting it's due in an hour. Need to drop your car off to get the tires rotated? She'll be happy to give you a ride home. Except that she'll either forget to pick you up or get lost on the way. It's a wonder that this one's brain generates enough electricity to make her walk.

Smile, bobble a friendly nod, but keep walking if you happen to run into this one.

Swimming further down this muddy stream is the Permanent Victim. She'll *always* have a bad boss, mean husband, and bratty kids. Her lawyer cheats her, her doctor misdiagnosed her latest ailment, and her lowlife brother just borrowed her last $20.

She's seems so nice, and so brave in dealing with her miserable life, that you can't help but like her. You empathize with her. You make friends. You listen, and listen, and listen. After a while you get the distinct feeling you're watching repeats of a daytime soap. That's because PV is addicted to suffering.

She's another of the zodiac's passive/aggressive warriors. The way she tries to control you and everyone around her is by acting so selfless that you feel compelled to come to her aid. At first, you'll offer advice. Soon you'll offer the name of a good therapist. Finally, you'll offer to buy her a ticket back home so that you can get her the hell out of your life.

Shark-bite Shirley is the worst of the worst. Being the old bitch-um-soul that she is, Shirley's been around the zodiac wheel before. She picked up all the traits of the bad girls in each of the other signs and shoved them into a package of all-time new lows.

Shirley is dangerous because she's into power plays that hurt people for the fun of it. She'll try to come between you and your man, or best friend, to eventually dump on them the way she dumped on you.

At work, she gossips incessantly. It's hard to not get suckered in, because as do the other rotten Fish, she comes on as all sweetness and light. However, this one's a true bottom feeder who thinks nothing of destroying someone's rep if she can gain something, even if it's only the personal satisfaction of seeing the other person suffer. She won't care if it's the truth as long as it's juicy news.

When she's on a roll, Shirley can outmaneuver the sneakiest Crab and play more head games than the most paranoid Gemini. The best way to avoid getting bitten is to cut a wide berth around her. Don't let her trap you into having lunch. Don't join her on break for the latest grapevine newsflash. Don't ever believe a word she says, and for God's sake, never confide one thing in this woman.

Bondability

Sister of the soul: Capricorn, Sagittarius, Aquarius
Inner circle: Taurus, Gemini, Libra, Scorpio
Party pal: Leo, Cancer, Pisces, Aries
Casual chum: Virgo
Famous Pisces friendship: Jessica Biel and Scarlett Johansson (a Sagittarius)

Venus in Pisces

Astrologically, Venus is said to be exalted in Pisces. Venus's traits of compassion, sensitivity, and devotion are magnified in the spiritual sign of Pisces. This girlfriend will often have musical talent that can lead to a career in composing, singing, or teaching.

Pisces Venus adds a self-sacrificing aspect to every Sun sign. It also adds an edge of gullibility and neediness to the strongest Sun. This girlfriend lives for love and acceptance. She can often become dependent in her relationships and can be the pal who seems to have more than her share of crises. She can fall for the wrong kind of guy or get suckered in by a con artist who'll drain her bank account. The most practical Taurus or logical Aquarius will follow her heart in relationship matters, even when her head is screaming that she's making a huge mistake. Illusion overrules her common sense sometimes, because this Venus sees the world through those metaphorical rose-colored glasses.

Illusion rules her beauty style too. Pisces Venus will use any and all tricks from makeup to plastic surgery to maintain her façade of youth. She'll take risks on new procedures and try every over-the-counter, youth-restoring cosmetic on the market. She can be so skilled at applying her makeup that no matter how many layers she's piled on, she achieves a natural, flawless look.

The Venus Pisces fashion style is romantic. Every Sun sign with this placement will have more than a few outfits made of silky, semi-sheer fabrics or glittery, sequined tops and velvet skirts.

Moon in Pisces

The Pisces Moon adds a strong desire to make the world a better place to every Sun sign. However, it isn't the most realistic Moon sign in the Universe. The Pisces Moon sees things the way it feels they should be, rather than the way they are.

This Moon child is optimistic in the face of insurmountable odds, and has an almost magical way of pulling success out of imminent defeat. A Pisces Moon brings more than a touch of intuition to any Sun, and can make the native truly psychic when in the Sun signs of Gemini, Cancer, Scorpio, and Pisces. Her emotions are deep, loyal, and discreet. The most unthinking Sun sign will be much more prone to keeping secrets with this placement.

A Pisces Moon chum can be full of anxiety and nameless fears. She has an overworked emotional imagination that can lean toward a negative outlook. Generally, though, this girlfriend is wise, empathetic, and a friend to everyone.

The illusionist in the Pisces Moon can enhance either the negative or positive traits of any Sun sign. For example, it can make an Aries even more meddlesome or a Gemini so flaky she can never be counted on. It can also lighten up the pessimistic side of Virgo and bestow a sunny, humorous disposition on Scorpio.

A Pisces Moon helps the Air signs touch the emotions of others as well as boosting their intuitive powers. In Earth, it brings insight and imagination. The Fire signs have more depth of emotion, and the Water signs will usually have some sort of unusual artistic talent.

Your Pisces Guy Pal

He's sensitive, sweet, imaginative, and a little lazy. A Pisces buddy is another man who makes lifelong friendships. He's a guy who can talk for hours about anything from world affairs to his latest dating disaster. He has opinions, but he won't force them on you. He has a wild side and witty humor, which makes him great to take almost anywhere.

He will never admit it, but he has a rich fantasy life that occasionally might include you. He won't act on it unless you make the first move. Don't do it if you want to keep his friendship. A Pisces guy's love life is as messy as a Scorpio's. If you're hurting, he'll let you cry on his shoulder and give you surprisingly good advice. He's another guy who will tell you when he's having girl trouble.

You can count on him to help you in any way he can, whether it's picking you up at the airport or fixing a leaky faucet. This buddy usually has an artistic streak that could be anything from refinishing furniture to playing guitar. He's up for anything, from visiting the zoo, to visiting a theme park, to riding roller coasters all day. A Pisces guy is kind of like Peter Pan. He hates to grow up. That's why he's so much fun.

About the Author

Hazel Dixon-Cooper is *Cosmopolitan*'s Bedside Astrologer and the author of the internationally bestselling astrology books *Born on a Rotten Day* and *Love on a Rotten Day*. She also writes the daily horoscopes for *CosmoMobile* and can be heard every Friday morning on *Wake Up with Cosmo* on Sirius Satellite Radio, for the latest celebrity gossip and weekend astro forecast. A resident of California, Hazel is a professional astrologer and a research member of the American Federation of Astrologers.

To Our Readers

Weiser Books, an imprint of Red Wheel/Weiser, publishes books across the entire spectrum of occult and esoteric subjects. Our mission is to publish quality books that will make a difference in people's lives without advocating any one particular path or field of study. We value the integrity, originality, and depth of knowledge of our authors.

Our readers are our most important resource, and we appreciate your input, suggestions, and ideas about what you would like to see published. Please feel free to contact us, to request our latest book catalog, or to be added to our mailing list.

Red Wheel/Weiser, LLC
500 Third Street, Suite 230
San Francisco, CA 94107
www.redwheelweiser.com